Proposal for a New College

by

Peter Abbs

Lecturer in Education, University of Sussex

and

Graham Carey

Senior Lecturer in Art, Bingley College of
Education

HEINEMANN EDUCATIONAL BOOKS
LONDON

Heinemann Educational Books Ltd
22 Bedford Square, London WC1B 3HH
LONDON EDINBURGH MELBOURNE AUCKLAND
HONG KONG SINGAPORE KUALA LUMPUR NEW DELHI
IBADAN NAIROBI JOHANNESBURG
EXETER (NH) KINGSTON PORT OF SPAIN

ISBN 0 435 80013 2

© Peter Abbs and Graham Carey 1977

First published 1977

Reprinted 1979

For those who will follow and especially for Hannah, Emily, Annabel, Miranda, Theodore.

Typeset in 10/11pt Garamond by
Spectrum Typesetting and printed in
Great Britain by Biddles of Guildford
Martyr Road, Guildford, Surrey

Yet how to begin? How to show
The living together of men
That it may be understood
And become a world that can be mastered
. . . the great art of living together?

Brecht

It requires a totally new attitude of mind to be able to look away from the present educational institutions to the strangely different ones that will be necessary for the second or third generation. At present the labours of higher education produce merely the savant or the official or the business man or the Philistine or, more commonly, a mixture of all four; and the future institutions will have a harder task;—not in itself harder, as it is really more natural, and so easier; and further, could anything be harder than to make a youth into a savant against nature, as now happens?—But the difficulty lies in unlearning what we know and setting up a new aim; it will be an endless trouble to change the fundamental idea of our present education system . . . It is already time to put these objects before us; for some generation must begin the battle, of which a later generation will reap the victory. The solitary man who has understood the new fundamental idea of culture is at the parting of the ways.

Nietzsche

Contents

I
Challenge and Response

It is only possible to answer for the final truth of principles, not for the direct success of plans. What can be immediately accomplished is always questionable; what can be finally accomplished, inconceivable.

Ruskin

I

In this book we propose the urgent need for a new college; a college which has been prefigured by many illustrious forerunners; a college whose aim is to integrate, for our own time and in the most demanding manner, the experiences of living and learning, of community and culture; a college which through its methods and habits may help to quietly usher in that post-industrial society on which the continuation and development of life must now depend; a college which nowhere exists and which, in the encompassing wilderness of our educational institutions, calls out to be created.

We are well aware that to turn to education as to a source of renewal has become one of the stock responses of our times, a liberal gesture as pious as it is empty. We too have heard critics, who proliferate as the light wanes, turn to education, crassly regarding it as a simple organ for social improvement. Our own society has become obsessed by the word 'education'. If there is something missing or remiss, then it is automatically suggested that education will remedy the fault. The schools must correct the society. And yet, ironically enough, the request that education rectify our social mistakes is not usually made by teachers but more often by liberal commentators, writers, journalists, academic researchers and politicians, people who since leaving their sixth form have never been inside a school. The request lacks all context. It rises up from a vacuum. But, then, the very word 'education' seems to hold within itself such healing energies that one has only to raise the magic word and the middle classes are convinced that something has been done or will be done. Schools, colleges, polytechnics, universities—they will answer the problems.

But which schools? Which colleges? Which polytechnics? Which universities? Indeed which institutions in our society can be identified with a genuine educational process? And, to raise a further question, what constitutes a genuine educational process? These are the perplexing questions which, hidden beneath the journalistic patter for educational reform, must be released if we are to understand the possible ways in which a specific school or specific college—not schools, not colleges, for no deep change can happen on such a vast collective scale—might prefigure a community predicated on human values and authentic needs. The proposal that we make, then, is different from those commonly heard. In one sense, it is dramatically limited and tangible. We propose, in the first instance, *one* educational centre, one place in which to establish a creative form of education, one place in which to embody also that cultural and ecological alternative to our society which many are now, with great difficulty and much confusion, seeking. In another sense, the proposal is broad for it intends to erect that college on the firm ground of abiding educational and ecological principles.

Our belief in the need for such a college is not part of that stock response of a generation which calls for more and more collective education in the banal assumption that this alone will heal the state of our diseased civilization. We have been inside too many schools and colleges to support such abstract nonsense. Our conviction is rather that the vast majority of schools and colleges mirror our society so accurately that they too have lost touch with human purposes and are, at the moment, incapable of the necessary transformation. It seems to us that the only way forward is to found an autonomous small-scale residential college centred mainly on the teaching of the expressive and domestic arts and the humanities. We have little doubt that such a college, sympathetic to historic culture, drawing on present creative energies and anticipating the shape of things to come, would draw to itself a number of distinguished teachers who find they can no longer teach with heart in the bureaucratic and mass institutions in which they find themselves unwillingly imprisoned.

II

The problem with most of our schools, colleges, polytechnics and universities is that they seem incapable of representing any coherent body of values, or even one coherent form of pedagogy. There is no longer any immediate concensus as to what ultimately counts in education; in fact nothing matters, and anything goes. Institutions, to avoid the friction and anxiety aroused by fundamental discussion of ends (one of the great sources of intellectual and moral development), tend to smother these deep ethical and philosophical differences and endeavour to create a working unity by purely focusing on technical and mechanical goals. This policy of evasion has had disastrous consequences. It has meant that within places ostensibly devoted to the development of understanding, the various disciplines of knowledge have disintegrated, each developing, in isolation, its own pedagogy or, often, pedagogies. It has meant that most educational institutions have failed to create within their frameworks any sense of community, for any sense of cohesion they are able to achieve is based not on that power of imagination which is able to embrace and transcend human conflict but on mere organization, which is not. It has also meant that on the immense moral, political and spiritual issues of the day our schools and universities have remained, without exception, terrifyingly blank.

Nor has the driving effort to construct an egalitarian system of education helped to fill the peculiar philosophical emptiness of our educational institutions. On the contrary, it has contributed to it. In vociferously insisting on the right of every child to the same education, the conventional Left has overlooked the prior question as to what constitutes authentic educational activity. In struggling to make the present system just and open, it has, perhaps unintentionally, extended and reinforced the prevalent dreary utilitarian concepts of learning. Now every child has the same opportunity to be dulled by studying for a standard six 'O' levels. Equal education for all has become only certification for all. More radical and far-seeing images of education have become dimmed in the turmoil of administrative reorganization. It is pertinent to our theme to note here how incisive experiments within the state system of secondary education, the experiments made by Michael Duane in England, by Robert Mackenzie in Scotland, by Ray German in Wales, have all been stifled through heavy bureaucratic manoeuvres.

In the higher section of education, during the last ten years, we have witnessed the emergence of a new system of giant polytechnics, huge multi-purpose, multi-campus institutions, modelled on commercial businesses, built unfeelingly of concrete slabs and glass. In many ways these educational complexes also represent an organized flight from the delicate tasks and paradoxes which mark true teaching and true learning, a flight into the unambiguous simplicities of mass and number. From the beginning, the preoccupation of the polytechnics was with what is, significantly, called 'recruitment'. In an attempt to 'recruit' the number of students allocated, one London polytechnic advertised itself using a semi-pornographic photograph, heading it with the sexually suggestive caption: 'Don't just stand there—Do something!'[1] Into what depths of ugliness our higher educational system seems ready to plunge for *numbers*! According to *The Times Educational Supplement* the widespread failure 'to recruit' was one of the main reasons for closing a number of colleges of education. This, it claimed, was 'a way to bump up binary student numbers towards their polytechnic targets'.[2]

The student power vaunted in the advertisement we have just quoted would, behind that thick smoke screen of 'liberation' (colour supplement-style), seem to reside in little more than the tyranny of number. We are deeply opposed to such abstract power, such anonymous energy. The power we would uphold is the power, not of opposed and schizoid collectivities—students against staff, staff against students, *us* and *them*—but of collaborative democracy. But such democracy, if it is to be the sensitive agent for self-understanding and social transformation, depends absolutely *on the deliberate constriction of numbers*. Just as there are precise limits to industrial growth, so there must be fairly definite limits of size to the maintaining of genuine and full-blooded democracy. A college of 200 could be truly democratic in its social structure, a college of 2,000, let alone 20,000, never.* In a polytechnic consisting of thousands of students, hundreds of teachers with their labouring proletariat of secretaries, cooks, cleaners, technical assistants, caretakers, porters and so on, it would be impossible to hold a dignified democratic meeting, let alone a continuous series of such meetings in which difficulties were freely aired, suggestions discussed, decisions taken. In truth, these desolate glass and concrete institutions have little choice but to be bureaucratic; little choice but to leave the student with the dominant impression that, in the eyes of his chosen place of study, he is little more than a cipher on the computer; little choice but to shatter the ideal unity of knowledge and culture into endlessly dividing and subdividing parts. Furthermore the upkeep of such large buildings entails immense costs, costs which are spiralling so rapidly that many local authorities are now at a loss as to how to meet them. Already, in so short a time, the brand new polytechnics seem like institutions of the past, like dinosaurs become too heavy and cumbersome for sensitive life. They look back to a time of mindless imperialistic expansion, not forward to the organic, cultured and restrained communities of the future. The polytechnics' counterpart in the outside society is, of course, the giant factory, mass-producing endless quantities of the same product for purchase on the consumer market. That factory, and the consumer market it both creates and serves, is also quickly approaching, for ecological, economic and spiritual reasons, the point of exhaustion and collapse. If the polytechnic is educating at all, it is educating for a

---

* The University of Berkeley, California, has around 30,000 students. It is of significance that it was this university which experienced some of the most extreme riots in the 1960s.

On the question of numbers, we are anxious not to be misunderstood. In principle we do not see any reason to withhold higher education from anyone who passionately seeks it. Moreover, since the cost of maintaining the polytechnics and universities has become prohibitive, we would suggest that our proposal for small-scale, self-managing colleges would, if it were to be nationally extended, provide a proper pattern of higher education, one even within reach of a bankrupt country.

society that, perhaps even in our own life time, will have ceased to exist.

A more interesting attempt to pioneer a new form of education has been made by the Open University. It must have brought the expressive and intellectual disciplines to many sensitive individuals who, for various reasons, had not had the chance of a university training, and who found themselves increasingly isolated in their own society. Any form of true intellectual and cultural liberation is not to be underestimated and we would not wish to disparage the means by which it came. And yet, in defining the purposes of the new college, we find ourselves deeply opposed to the general direction taken by the Open University. According to one prospectus, it claimed it was:

> open as to places . . . has no cloisters—a word meaning closed. Hardly even shall we have a campus. By a very happy chance, our only local habitation will be in the new city that is to bear two of the widest-ranging names in the history of English thought, Milton Keynes. But this is only where the tip of our toe touches ground. The rest of the University will be disembodied and airborne. From the start, it will flow all over the United Kingdom . . .[3]

'Disembodied and airborne', the spurious prose conjures up first and foremost, an image of Batman. We also find ourselves pondering the intellectual weight of a university which can, in such a breezy tone of voice, claim Keynes to be one 'of the widest-ranging names in the history of English thought'. More profoundly, where the Open University sees virtue in diffusion, we see merit in concentration. In a society so remorselessly propagating the shallow values of hedonistic pleasure and aimless consumption we defend the need for 'cloisters', for sheltered spaces, and believe in the making of an enclave within which the pursuits of culture can be timelessly and lovingly pursued, free from distraction. If, as we will claim throughout this book, education is essentially an activity of consciousness, engendered within a sustained relationship between mentor and student, then the need for a secure and appropriate meeting-place, becomes no trivial matter to be lightly dismissed. The act of teaching, protected by walls and actually enhanced by this enclosure, lies at the heart of the educational process. Great teachers are those who, not consciously but more by the unconscious power of their very presence, are able to release nascent intellectual and emotional elements in their students and to release these sometimes so forcibly that the individual can experience the event as one of startling inward transformation. Later in the book we will examine the qualities of true teachers and the important restricted contexts in which they teach. Here it must suffice to emphasize the ways in which the college we propose contrasts with the Open University. We, unlike the Open University, place the teaching process—that engaging experience of probing question, of tentative answer, of mutual collaboration, of individual unfolding and becoming—at the centre of education. But we also place the high art form of active teaching into the enduring context of community life, a context which includes the heavy, though community-shared, responsibility of running one's own society, both at the practical level of tasks to be performed and the political level of making democratic decisions about the nature and direction of the college itself. Our concern is to restore a broken unity, to recreate, though at a different level, something of that harmony, ceremony and order which characterize the timeless primitive community. How different this is from choosing one course of study with the Open University, where applicants are sent a number of printed forms which they are to use to communicate by post with a distant tutor! Airborne or not, such structures, in the end, promote only another variety of alienation, making what is desiccated and abstract seem normal and, therefore, desirable.

Those on the more extreme or disillusioned Left might, at this point, draw our attention to deschooling and the Anti-universities. We suspect that these movements have received so much attention in the educational press because, while remaining strangely elusive, they sound so 'progressive' that they can be given endless publicity, journalistic puffs and panegyrics, without there ever being any question of serious commitment or, even worse, application. About the Anti-university we would say that lacking permanence, being brief and spasmodic in nature, it must inevitably deteriorate into a frenetic and inverted establishment. Such an establishment may draw the headlines, but therein lies its very failure, for education—as we conceive it—is a prolonged and exacting discipline, inwardly releasing (at best) but outwardly undramatic and not, decidedly *not*, 'newsworthy'. For this reason the quest for community and creativity in our experimental college would be closed to the mass-media 'probes' and 'investigations'; an adventure of the spirit ceases to be real when it becomes too self-conscious, or when it becomes the subject-matter for effete intellectual titter on aimless Sunday mornings. Should the camera crews and journalists arrive, we would quietly show them the door.

With regard to deschooling, we would merely say that our society in its present state is so hostile to the gentle growth of intellect and feeling and the cultured community on which it must ultimately depend, that instead of demolishing our schools and thus leaving children defenceless before the commercial educators, we should rather work to convert those schools into creative centres. To deschoolers we suggest *re*schooling. This, as we have made clear, is easy to say *and not to mean*. At the present moment, the voices for humanity are so dispersed, so inwardly divided, that it is impossible to see how such a transmutation of our schools could take place. This is why we reject the liberal formulae for more education as fatuous. Those who proffer such formulae seem incapable of grasping the immense proportions of the crisis now confronting us. The long-term aim of our college is to pioneer a fresh model for educational practice, a model which would be cultural in aspiration, democratic in structure and ecological in organization. If the college can establish itself it will send out, like a strong plant, new runners into the world. Our answer, then, to deschoolers is that we need neither less education nor more, but *different forms of education*, forms which will hold within themselves the shape of tomorrow's world as our imagination, source of all living images and, therefore, of hope, would want it to be. The college we propose exists to elaborate one such prophetic form.

Finally, because one of the purposes of the new college is to train teachers—and we use the word 'train' quite deliberately—we must glance at our colleges of education, now in such a sad state of depletion and disarray. As early as 1932, L.C. Knights in an article published in *Scrutiny*, indicated that what were then called 'training colleges' were failing to nurture sensitive, articulate and committed teachers. In that article Knights claimed:

. . . the problem presented by the training colleges cannot be considered apart from the general state of English culture at the present time . . . Behind the educational system stands the cinema, newspapers, book societies and 'Big Business'—the whole machinery of 'Democracy' and standardization—so that the main charge against the training colleges is that they do nothing to foster such interests as their students possess, nothing to encourage an adult sense of responsibility. Their studies leave them perfectly fitted to their environment, perfectly unfitted for the work which they should do.[4]

Over forty years later this trenchant criticism remains pertinent, perhaps even more applicable now, with all the 'advances' in the electronic media, than when it was first written.

We ourselves have observed how in the colleges each new batch of students, rather passive in disposition, rather conformist in outlook, quietly settle down to the sober and organized routine of lectures and essays. Our students seem to arrive with the hidden assumption that education consists in little more than the steady accumulation and assimilation of facts, figures and quotations; an expectation which, on the whole, the colleges are more than ready to accept. Thus the habits of study engendered by second-rate sixth forms become, by implication, the accepted norm for all educational activity. This cerebral life of note-taking and note-reproducing will continue to the end of the course only to be disturbed in some cases, by anxieties relating to a difficult teaching-practice or, perhaps, a broken love affair. In our experience, the vast majority of students do not become passionately identified with or absorbed by their studies. Their own latent powers of thought, feeling and imagination will remain severed from the academic work they are given. For the release of emotion, for the shaping of phantasy, they will turn, uncritically, to their own inadequate resources, to pop-music, to discos, to popular television, to illiterate magazines, to trite newspapers and to trendy or sensational paperbacks. In other words, the education of their inner life will continue to be conducted by the cheapest of cultures manufactured and organized on a scale unknown in history. Thus after three years, the students will leave the college for their first teaching posts in, to quote again from L.C. Knights' excellent article, a state of 'arrested juvenility, of habituation to routine and a meek acceptance of the status quo'. That the colleges see no conflict between education and mass-culture, that they remain complacent before the dangerous division between knowledge and culture, between dry fact and debased feeling, is in itself a massive indictment of the whole system.

It is true, and must be quickly added, that there *are* students who, in our experience, do not become so successfully anaesthetized. These students are generally older, more articulate, more mature in judgement, more independent in mind. They have often come to the college keenly anticipating their main course only to be deeply disappointed by the mock academicism of their tutors who, often lacking the intellectual distinction of their university counterparts, are on the defensive, prickly before the challenge of questions and incapable of either initiating true collaborative study or of responding warmly to individual judgements and independent research. Even if the mature student does choose a main subject which is taught with imaginative sweep, intellectual rigour and generosity of feeling, he will find his interest battered on all sides by a ceaseless demand for 'work-units' from other and completely unrelated departments. He will be unable to devote his entire energy for a sustained period of time on any one elected pursuit. It is revealing and pertinent to note that the university student who is not diverted by a host of other academic commitments, has yet 35-40 per cent more time for personal study than the student from the college of education. It is as if the pragmatic philosophy of the colleges demands that their students, incapable of coping with prolonged periods of concentration, must be kept busy *in all directions and at all costs*. The multi-point examination profile with its miscellaneous assortment of components may be popular among staff for this very reason. And yet, the local university, which often regulates and assesses these profiles, would never tolerate for a single day in their own institutions, such a heterogeneous bag of academic tit-bits.

The syllabus and timetable of the typical college of education symbolizes a certain narrow attitude to education; it would seem to suggest that education is a matter of being busy, endlessly engaged, no matter what; that it is a matter of passive and correct assimilation; that the activity is essentially impersonal, standing erect above the turbulent (and creative) stream of inner life and outside the intricate web of human relationships; that, in sum, education is a matter of simple intellectual conformity rather than a personal reaching up for truth, integrity and wholeness of being. It is not altogether surprising, then, that the more mature and intelligent students who in their first months often come to their courses with a receptive enthusiasm, invariably end their days at college in a state of abulia, or, if not abulia, armoured cynicism. And in this mood they go out to teach the young!

Nearly all the major reports, whether commissioned or uncommissioned, whether the works of committees or concerned individuals, have found the colleges of education wanting, wanting in their main courses (particularly in the sciences), wanting in their professional courses, wanting in their relationship to the surrounding schools, wanting in their own intellectual and cultural life. By critical consent, the colleges have been bastions of mediocrity. In his own analysis of teacher-training published in *Fit to Teach*, Nicholas Bagnall summarizes the case we too have been making as follows:

> A picture begins to emerge of stagnant-minded and conformist students in stagnant and conformist colleges. The NFER in a note to the Select Committee was disturbed by 'the apparent lack of any signs of significant curriculum development in the colleges themselves'.[5]

The note which Bagnall quotes continues:

> 'The basic structure of the college course has changed little since the war. Even the introduction of the three-year course—an obvious opportunity for radical revision—seemed to result in merely the recrystallization of the former pattern, in spite of the many discussions and controversies, which preceeded the change.'

The comment helps to explain why L.C. Knights' criticism with which we began this brief analysis has remained impressively relevant and continues to be so in spite of recent re-organization.

In condemning the education provided by the typical college of education—and we grant there are exceptions—it does not follow that we approve of the present attempt to re-arrange the system through a series of ill-considered closures, amalgamations and mergers.* As we will suggest in the final chapter, the colleges *do* possess many essential elements—elements of scale, size, habitat—which we must not abandon. Furthermore, an effort to create a new administrative order will, in the absence of deeper meanings and informing aims, only engender further confusion and, even worse, create a psychic paralysis among teachers, tutors and students. What is needed—and the need is desperate—is an influx of broad philosophical ideas and conceptions.

III

It requires an uncommonly emancipated mind to envisage those educational institutions that will be necessary for the next century. What seems certain is that these institutions will grow up out of a configuration of concepts, values and convictions quite alien to our own. This brings us to our concern with an aesthetic education. The emphasis in these pages will fall on the arts and humanities. This is so for a number of reasons. Firstly, our own teaching, and therefore whatever authority we may possess, has been within the arts: in pottery, art and film; in literature, philosophy and autobiography. Put bluntly, we are not equipped or qualified to discuss the teaching of science. Secondly, we believe that the full meaning of an aesthetic and creative education has not been generally understood and is still regarded by many, who should know better, as a mode of therapy, a harmless releasing of suppressed libido, a matter of uninhibited self-expression. In contrast, we see a training in the arts as an initiation into the discipline of forms in which the seeming antithesis of tradition and innovation, of construct and

---

* It is claimed that the new Diploma in Higher Education has improved courses and that students are now working more profitably within them. We would contend that studies which under the unit system have to be developed in nine months will tend to lose their depth and under the pressures of time become peculiarly rigid or merely schematic. The cultivation of consciousness and the general acquisition of skills on which this depends is not a task to be hurried or, indeed, completely programmed. The best education is secured where demanding studies are grounded in a student-tutor relationship sustained over a number of years and supported, beyond that, by a true and encompassing community life.

expression, of restraint and freedom, are fused into a higher, and therefore truer, synthesis. For us, a creative discipline entails not only the power to express but also the power to control, to give shape and order to the flux of immediate consciousness—it is a view we intend to clarify in Chapter 3.

Thirdly, in our view, scientific enquiry, with its empirical and mathematical procedures, cannot adequately meet the existential and so, compelling questions raised by human existence. The deep questions that rise up from within, turning our own natures into riddles and enigmas—such questions as 'Who am I?' and 'How can I become that which I am?'—cannot begin to be answered or even (at the moment) adequately comprehended by the scientific disciplines.* They can only be elaborated, celebrated, explored and interpreted through the symbolic and communal discourse of Art and through a continuous study of the Humanities, humanly conceived. The delicate study of symbol and meaning would, therefore, be the focal point of our college's academic and creative studies. When we are witnessing in industrial society the relentless suppression of the ontological dimension, the value of such a commitment to existential understanding and imaginative recreation cannot be too highly esteemed. It is commonplace now to find many of those irreducibly human questions, relating to existential meaning, cunningly transposed into technical problems and, then, falsely solved. Such a steady and ubiquitous process of reductive interpretation and crude extrapolation must culminate in man seeing himself as little more than an assemblage of functions, drives, components; parts which can be easily taken apart and reassembled according to the dictates of fashion or the needs of the industrial estate. Only the philosophical and creative discovery or rediscovery of man *as being*, can halt this movement and prevent that human catastrophe which, if unchecked, it must lead to—for life follows in the track of concepts and images.

There is a further and related historical reason for our decision to concentrate on the creative Arts and the Humanities in the new

---

* We will suggest later that science is, in fact, a symbolic construct of the mind and includes aesthetic elements. At the moment, however, a great deal of scientific study is still based on an outmoded view of 'objectivity' which, as we shall see, derives from the seventeenth-century philosophers.

College. Here we can only sketch, in swift, dramatic strokes, the nature of this reason.* Since about the beginning of the seventeenth century, the dominant energy of man's mind has been turned outwards upon the world. That gaze has been analytical rather than contemplative; aggressive rather than loving; and it has been masculine, far removed, that is, from those essentially feminine impulses to cherish, to revere and to reflect. Darwin in his *Autobiography* testified to the particular limitations inherent in that disposition of mind when he wrote:

> But now for many years I cannot endure to read a line of poetry; I have tried lately to read Shakespeare, and found it so intolerably dull that it nauseated me. I have also lost any taste for pictures or music . . . *My mind seems to have become a kind of machine for grinding general laws out of large collections of fact*, but why this should have caused the atrophy of that part of the brain alone, on which *the higher tastes depend*, I cannot conceive . . . The loss of these tastes is a loss of happiness, *and may possibly be injurious to the intellect, and more probably to the moral character, by enfeebling the emotional part of our nature*. [Our italics]

As we now know, this insistent limited form of intentionality, disregarding historic culture and introspection alike, was characteristic of the Enlightenment mentality and resulted in seeing the creation as blind, devoid of mind and telic purpose, driven either by the impersonal laws of matter and motion or, in the case of evolutionary theory, the mechanisms of instinct darkly fighting for survival. Perhaps if Darwin's intentionality had been broader, if it had been illuminated by his 'higher tastes' for Shakespeare, art and music, it would have perceived another universe, or rather, the same universe in another way, and as a result constructed an infinitely richer theory of evolution. We cannot know. But the speculation—and it is no more than that—directs us to the fact that the scientific theories which have had such an influence on our consciousness were made by men who quite deliberately excluded elements of subjectivity, of feeling,

---

* We realize how lightly we are about to skate over immense depths and diverse currents, and ask those readers who want to consult more solid matter supporting our case to consult the appropriate bibliography.

phantasy, intuition and culture from their examination of nature. This exclusion can now be seen to constitute a particular bias, a predisposition to reject the subjective dimension as an actual part of the manifold we call life. From the time of Galileo onwards, the philosophers of science and its many practitioners tended to deny inward space and inward time. They denigrated, in effect, all that spoke of the mysterious inwardness of man-within-nature. Their gaze upon the world's surfaces was, as we have said, rigidly masculine. It was the early empiricist Francis Bacon who, that knowledge might be won, recommended chaining Nature to 'the rack' that she might be examined 'with levers and with screws'. The genders we find ourselves using here, masculine scientist and feminine nature, are, we believe, not only of semantic interest but of the profoundest significance. Nor can there be little doubt that the exploration of physical space—the discovery of vast oceans and immense unknown land-masses, the discovery of new flora and fauna, of precious stones, minerals and a surplus of materials hitherto undreamed of—coinciding with the rise of science, reinforced its powerful, if exclusive, frame of reference, providing it with all the qualities of high drama, of adventure and of conquest.

To Faustian Man, for ever scanning far horizons, for ever prizing open the gift of nature, the possibilities for material existence must have seemed limitless. At least, until the second part of our own century. It is not our purpose to document all the ways in which the planet was opened out, the dramatic way in which the globe was given its objective contours, those contours that we now take so much for granted, as if all men had seen the same world as we do. Nor is it our intention to describe how that ancient and intricate pattern of spatially-constricted and timeless primitive communities was ruthlessly effaced—though its bearing on our argument must be painfully clear. We are concerned only to draw attention to *the mode of consciousness* which informed that remarkable quest for objective knowledge and external power. In short, we are not so much interested in the epistemology of scientific investigation, but in the psychology that, historically, accompanied it, a psychology that became with the industrial revolution, the psychology of our whole civilisation.

One example is, perhaps, revealing, for it indicates how all-pervasive was the shift in consciousness. Until the Renaissance, few individuals had thought of deriving pleasure from wilfully pitting themselves against nature by scaling her barest and highest peaks. For centuries before (and after), within the unity conferred by another culture, the Chinese had taken delight in delicately painting the mist-shrouded tops of their own mountains so that they appeared like the ethereal emanations of spiritual energy. It had to wait till the sixteenth century, for European man to regard these beautiful forms as obstacles to be conquered by the force of will, the indomitable power of the masculine mind.

That great adventure of Western consciousness into outer space is now effectively over. In our own life time our planet has become alarmingly small and, simultaneously, more heavily populated. There is little remaining space to tempt the appetite of the individual explorer. The world is closing in on us. In our sprawling cities of cement and glass, life moves to the quiet hands of the clock, measuring two spans of organized time, one for production, the other for consumption; work and leisure. Even the recent conquests of distant matter, passively watched by millions on their colour television screens, are achievements more of the computer than the independent pioneer. A human being now walking on the moon's distant face is said to perform 'extra-vehicular activity'. A recent Russian expedition to Everest was described as a success 'coming from logistical capability and space-age planning'. In all outward pursuits—and in this we would include scientific exploration—the audacity of the explorer, the dedication and will-power of the pioneer, have given way to 'expertise', 'group co-ordination', 'computer feedback', all dependent on state planning, finance and approval. Qualities of character have become curiously dated. Collective civilization can find no room for them.

Born into a contracting world, the mind has no choice but to create another theme. Where will it be found? Or, rather, where *can* it be found? That aspect of the world contained in Descartes' concept of 'extended matter' has been chartered and squared, and as Hopkins pointed out long before the ecologists, 'seared with trade' and 'smeared with toil'. Where can it be found but in that inward domain from which we have become sadly estranged? And, as the Romantics, from Wordsworth to Lawrence, have persisted in maintaining, there *are* other ways of relating to nature. She is so much more than 'extended matter'. If in the past an attitude of 'I over and against it' with its unconscious corollary 'It over and against me' has been generated, now a seemingly more comprehensive and a certainly more sensitive response of 'I within it' and more deeply, 'It within me' needs cultivating. Because we have discarded so much traditional guidance, because we have allowed our inheritance of life-wisdom incarnated in folk-culture, in religion, in myth, in ritual, in poetry, in carving, song and dance to wither and decay, we feel anxious and powerless before the immensity of the tasks now needed—indeed, now upon us. How can we recreate what for centuries we have been taught to regard as superstition or mere decoration? How are we to open those doors which turn not into the machine or the office block but into inner life? How in the hollow pit of the consumer society are we to build the ceremonial and cultural centre? These are disturbing questions. Any fulfilment they might promise seems beyond us, beyond our spiritual reach.

Seen on the other side of a wholly appropriate and in no way neurotic anxiety, these same questions constitute the challenge of the age. They imply risk. They involve a voyage into the unknown, into deep space, into indivisible duration. And as with all questions, they hold out the possibilities of disaster and of triumph. They would seem to be the cluster of questions which rise in the minds of a creative minority in the chaotic period between the demise of an external civilization and the birth of a new culture. Here, we claim, is the spiritual adventure of the next century. 'Another turn of the gyre', said Yeats, 'and myth', the symbolic language of the poetic mind so despised by the Enlightenment, 'is wisdom, pride, discipline'.[7] Such a dramatic transference of psychic energy from the collective and mechanical to the communal and cultural is not unique. We find instructive analogues in the past. When the Roman Empire had become little more than a vast mass of uncoordinated machinery and when the people of Rome, fed on state-provided corn and circuses, had turned the calamity of their own civilization into a perverted festival, a few tiny monasteries on the extreme peripheries of the Empire, often on islands (nature's enclaves) kept alight the flame of existential man and, more shrewdly, created the strong foundations of an alternative culture. It was in this same period of collective frenzy, when the energy of the age had contracted to the beats of mass sensation, that autobiography, that unique vehicle for sustained introspection and the construction of the private self, emerged. One senses, in these examples, a powerful dialectical relationship between the widespread forces working for collapse and the individual forces striving for transcendence and renewal. The Romantic movement likewise, was a critical and discerning response to the externalization of consciousness fostered by the industrial revolution. It is fascinating to note here that it was Shelley who in his *Defence of Poetry*—written over twenty years before Whewell coined the word 'scientist'—anticipated our present argument when he wrote:

> The cultivation of those sciences which have enlarged the limits of the Empire over the external world has, for want of the poetical faculty, proportionally circumscribed those of the internal world; and man, having enslaved the elements, remains himself a slave.

A similar argument was, of course, made by all the significant Romantic writers. It was given mythological beauty by Blake, a fierce polemical energy by Dickens, and in our own century it was given a fresh intensity by the novels of D.H. Lawrence and the poetry of Yeats:

> Locke sank into a swoon;
> The garden died;
> God took the spinning-jenny
> Out of his side.[8]

These indomitable rebellions of the creative minority—the Christian, the Romantic, the Existentialist rebellions—presage a social order that must eventually supersede the civilisation which, when measured against the needs of the whole man, has been condemned as pitifully inadequate. From these traditions of coherent protest, we must learn all we can.

The distinguished American economist, Robert Heilbroner, in *An Inquiry into the Human Prospect* contemplating the demise of the industrial state, recently wrote:

> What sort of society might eventually emerge? As I have said more than once, I believe the long-term solution requires nothing less than the gradual abandonment of the lethal

techniques, the uncongenial life-ways, and the dangerous mentality of industrial civilisation . . . This implies a sweeping reorganisation of the mode of production in ways that cannot be foretold, but that would seem to imply the end of the giant factory, the huge office, perhaps of the urban complex . . .

It is therefore possible that a post-industrial society would also turn in the direction of many pre-industrial societies—toward the exploration of inner states of experience rather than the outer world of fact and material accomplishment. Tradition and ritual . . . would probably once again assert their ancient claims as the guide to and solace for life . . . In our discovery of 'primitive' cultures, living out their timeless histories, we may have found the single most important object lesson for future man.[9]

D.H. Lawrence might have expressed the case more passionately but not more cogently. In Chapter 3, we will attempt to define exactly what we—and what our college—can learn from a study of primitive culture.

Such a transition to a pattern of stable communities, with the archetypal experiences of birth, growth, maturity, death, rebirth given dignity through the creation of shared symbols, will, according to Heilbroner, be neither inevitable nor easy. Considering the prevailing values of people today, he asks:

Will they not curse these future generations whose claims to life can be honoured only by sacrificing present enjoyments; and will they not, if it comes to a choice, condemn them to non-existence by choosing the present over the future?[10]

It is this choice and the catastrophe it will bring that we must, at all costs, avert. The challenge facing a genuinely experimental college couldn't be more momentous. Quite literally, the issues are those of life or death; resurrection or extinction.

Seen in a broad cultural and ecological context such as we have sketched in this chapter, the need for a new college, exploring and charting new connections between living and learning, between self and the world, between material frugality and joyous existence, becomes imperative. The great crisis we face demands not the further regimentation of consumer impulses, not further importation of advanced technology, not even more research, but, rather, a willingness to innovate, to begin small radical experiments, first-hand attempts to discover and *re*discover forms of relationship and creation which do not entail the squandering of depleted resources or require an ant-like collectivity with an alienated élite at the top and a degraded proletariat beneath. The task of the new college is to fashion that community which will restore man to himself, to his neighbour and to nature, on which he depends not only for healthy supplies of proper food but also for his sense of beauty, scale, rhythm and pattern. We find some hope in the fact that from the very beginning this has been one of the great traditional tasks of the living arts. It has also been one of the main purposes of a number of traditional communities and earlier experimental colleges—and it is to these that we now wish to turn our attention.

II
Antecedents

If education is to become what Coleridge thought it ought to be, 'that most weighty and concerning of all sciences', it must do so by an utter conversion here at its centre. It must become an inquiry, active and intimately personal, devoted to the interrogation of self, to all that is grounded in the self, and to that transformation of self hoped for in learning.

William Walsh

I

It is for their realization of what may strike the reader as utopian vision that we here invoke a few of the great and historically-tested institutions of education and community-living. Our selection of prototypes is personal. Our reading has not been methodical. Rather we have found ourselves being powerfully drawn to certain images, images which left their impress on our minds long after the books had been put down. In the writing of such men as Walter Daniel, Lewis Mumford, John Rice and Walter Gropius, we were reminded that education could stand for something more than is currently conceived by the word, could symbolize a process infinitely rich and strange. Through their words, and through the images those words released, we saw our proposal for a new college as an effort to crystallize, once again, for our own time and for our own distraught needs, 'the great good place'. Even man's first enclave, the cave itself, its walls enhanced by the play of art, seemed an early and partial embodiment of that cultured community we again sought to recreate. The great good places we briefly describe in this chapter belong to different ages and embody different cultural ideals but there remains beneath their legitimate diversity, a common pursuit, a unifying concept. This concept has been best defined by Lewis Mumford in his concise formulation of the Greek concept *paideia:*

> Paideia is education looked upon as a life-long transformation of the human personality, in which every aspect of life plays a part. Unlike education in the traditional sense, paideia does not limit itself to the conscious learning processes, or to inducting the young into the social heritage of the community. *Paideia is rather the task of giving form to the act of living itself:* treating every occasion of life as a means of self-fabrication, and as part of a larger process of converting facts into values, processes into purposes, hopes and plans into consummation and realisations. *Paideia is not merely a learning: it is a making and a shaping; and man himself is the work of art that paideia seeks to form.*[1] [Our italics]

The task of giving form to the act of living itself is what unifies our educational forerunners and makes them central to our theme. Even the physical efforts to construct the place, to make an enduring institution out of the passing and ephemeral impulses of life, represents a true manifestation of *paideia*. There is something heroic in the way thirteen monks set off from York to build Fountains Abbey. We find something humanly warm and gently touching in the custom agreed upon soon after the founding of Ruskin College where the cook (and in the early days *each* student had his turn at preparing meals) had 'to appear in the doorway of the dining-room half-way through the meal to receive the comments of his victims'. When we read in Martin Duberman's *Black Mountain College* how a distinguished academic staff laboured with their students to build a necessary extension, we experience a deep hope for man's unity. And we take heart when we hear Walter Gropius, shrewd founder of the Bauhaus, declare:

> You should be bold, you should have the courage to be Utopian, and think out certain things which it might be desirable for man to have, although in that moment you do not know whether you can do it. But if you trust that you can do extra-ordinary things, then comes the problem of how to reach that goal, and it should be reached in a very direct way, step by step, realistically. I think the Bauhaus idea had very much that is Utopian in it, but step by step we tried to realise it and we have given evidence that a group of people can work on such an idea and come to a certain

understanding which then radiates into other parts of the world.[2]

These are examples of the words and images we have been inspired by. They tempt us to assert that no definition of reality is complete until it includes life's possibilities and those sublime elusive aspirations to erect the good society, the cultural and ceremonial centre. Facts, as the etymology of the word reveals, are not given but made. We look back at the rich storehouse of communities in the past and find evidence for our convictions. Man makes the reality he believes in.

The accounts that follow do not pretend to be full descriptions. In wandering from one social artefact to the other, we found our minds concentrating on different facets. No doubt, we were half-consciously looking for those elements we wished to include in our new college—for the great achievements of the past are there not only for us to quietly admire but also to actively learn from. It is in the nature of a prototype that it provides those original forms from which further structures may be hammered out for the future.

II

Fountains Abbey / Rievaulx Abbey

How much can we infer from the records and remaining ruins of these great monastic foundations—foundations which preserved the continuity of culture and fostered the growth of scholarship, compassion and forgiveness?

The plan of Fountains Abbey shows an environment which was a complete embodiment of the aims of Cistercian life, both materially and symbolically. The close proximity of their parts and the intimate relationship between them was essential. Within the boundaries of these walls men were to spend their whole lives, living as members of one spiritual family. Only a tight cluster of buildings could promote such a concentrated and ordered life. Within the walls, everything had to be provided for, the needs of the body (the monastery was largely self-sufficient), the needs of the mind (the monastery would have a library, containing not only the works of the early Fathers of the Church, but also some of the Latin and Greek classics, Aesop, Aristotle, Plato, Homer; it would probably also have in its cloisters carrells where the novices kept their own chest of books and where they could privately withdraw to read and write), and the needs of the soul (the monastery was, as the timetable of daily worship shows, first and foremost a place for spiritual exaltation). In its severity and simplicity, the Cistercian order expressed a powerful *idea about life*, not only about its ultimate meaning but also about the way in which it should be lived. It sought to join together the quest for individual salvation and the need for community, the need for solitude and the need to belong. It wished not only to reconcile but to unify the economic, intellectual and spiritual aspirations of man and to provide the context and time-continuum in which this achievement could be sustained. The monastery thus came to provide for its members a balanced life. Each day gave ample time for reading, writing and discussion, time for physical labour—inside the building and outside in the gardens and fields—and time for worship, for inward prayer and the communal chanting of plainsong. The practice of self-sufficiency, ensuring that there was little anxiety as to physical want, freed the mind to concentrate on the finer matters of existence, that double task of living close to the primary sources of Being and of giving fine form to the act of living itself. And, although the abbot was considered as father to the family of monks and expected—and required—obedience, there was, at the same time, considerable freedom for the members to discuss matters relating to their own monastery. Every morning at Chapter the monks would gather together to discuss any problems that had arisen since the previous meeting. Here, too, matters of discipline were raised and, if necessary, public correction of faults given. Such a daily gathering must have given a delicately human and an almost democratic face to monastic life.

With these general reflections we turn to consider one remarkable abbot, Ailred of Rievaulx, who became head of that remote Yorkshire monastery in 1147. He was then thirty-seven years of age and held the office till he died early in 1167. During this period, Ailred's great gifts as an abbot and mentor came to maturity. He was, we are told by his contemporary biographer Walter Daniel (who was also a monk at Rievaulx), a man 'of extreme delicacy of feeling, condescending to the weakness of all, nor did he think that any who besought him for charity's sake should be saddened'. So—

In receiving those who desired to come to religion he made as though he would have gone further, that the prayers of the bretheren might press him, as one unwilling, to consent; hence it came about that many were received of whom he had no real knowledge, for he often left it to the judgement of the community to receive whom they would.[3]

A result of this 'condescension' was an enormous increase of the numbers at Rievaulx.*

Ailred's biographer, in a vivid phrase, describes the crowded church on feast days, when the majority of the conversi would be back from the granges, as packed with monks as closely as a hive of bees; so close, indeed, that they could not stir.

Ailred never tired of repeating that the singular glory of Rievaulx was that it had learnt, beyond all other houses, to bear with the weak and to have compassion for those in need.

All [he said], strong and weak alike, should find in Rievaulx a haven of peace, a spacious and calm home . . . of it should be said: Thither the tribes go up, the tribes of the Lord, unto the testimony of Israel, to give thanks unto the name of the Lord. Yea, tribes of the strong and of the weak. For that cannot be called a house of religion which spurns the weak, since: Thine eyes have seen mine imperfections and in thy book are all written.[4]

And so, as Walter Daniel declares, men drawn by the compassion and understanding of Ailred flocked to the monastic enclave at Rievaulx. The power of the attraction can only be understood by assuming that what the monks saw so nobly expressed in the abbot, an inner unity of existence, they passionately wished to attain for themselves. Nor did their expectations soar beyond the social reality, for Ailred, as we have seen, was aware of his own shadow ('Thine eyes have seen my imperfection and in thy book are all written') and, therefore, of other people's. If there was to be true spiritual advance, there had also to be failure and *the understanding of failure*. This creative

---

* If we may take as definitive Ailred's own figures and those of Walter Daniel, the community which in 1132 may have numbered only twenty-five had risen to three hundred by 1142 and to six hundred and fifty by 1165.

acceptance of regression marks Ailred out as one of the great teachers of his time—it does not, of course, mean that he condoned the actions that such regression might lead to. Once again, Walter Daniel in his biography points to the practical results of such a pedagogy of 'condescension':

> Was there ever anyone weak in body or character expelled from that house unless his evil ways gave *offence to the whole community* or ruined his own hope of salvation? Hence there came to Rievaulx from foreign nations and distant lands a stream of monks who needed brotherly mercy and true compassion, and there they found the peace and sanctity without which no man can see God. Yes, those who were restless in the world and to whom no religious house gave entry, coming to Rievaulx, the mother of mercy, and finding the gates wide open, freely entered therein. [5]

For Ailred, then, the monastery was no enclosed Eden in which only rare souls could find green pasture. Rather it was as catholic as the medieval church, a home for identities of every kind, a spiritual centre, preserving culture, refining consciousness. And it must not be forgotten that three out of every four who came were unlettered, stolid labourers. It is certain that of the choir-monks, many, no doubt the majority, were ordinary men with no obvious refinement or clear intellectual gifts. Yet all the sources reveal the existence alike at Rievaulx and the other houses of Ailred's family, of a numerous class of monks who had passed through the new humanist discipline of the schools and retained, within the framework of the Cistercian life of labour, silence and simplicity, a warm eagerness of mind and heart which few who now visit the ruins of Rievaulx would associate with its walls. It was with this group of monks, the intellectual élite who were nonetheless members of the general community, sharing the same tasks and burdens of the self-supporting monastery, that, we are told, Ailred's relations were the most penetrating and sustained. He stood at the centre of the group, his finger raised, asking the most penetrating of questions or quietly bringing another text to bear upon the enrapt discussion.

David Knowles in *Saints and Scholars* leaves us with the final impression of our medieval mentor:

> We see him, the Cistercian abbot, the centre of a group of listeners and interlocutors, engaged in one of those discussions half Platonic, half scholastic in character, which in one form or another absorbed for more than two centuries the interests and energies of so many in Western Europe.[6]

The heart of intellectual Europe beat inside these monastic enclaves. Many were remote—even more remote than Rievaulx—but there was nothing insular about them. They were of their time and in their time even as they pointed, with an assurance we no longer have, beyond it.

What can we learn from Rievaulx? We can learn from Ailred's example, his humanity, his openness to experience, his psychological acumen. We can learn much about the self-sufficient, self-managing, small-scale community.* We can learn a great deal from that incandescent image of unity, the Christ-man in whom the seeming opposites of work and study, solitude and community, of self and others, were brought harmoniously together. The monastery, at its best and before its sublime concept degenerated into the inertia of empty routine, symbolized and actually sustained the balanced life, the good life. In *The Myth of the Machine* Lewis Mumford, reflecting on the monastic order inspired by Saint Benedict, wrote:

> Probably the practical necessity to become self-supporting, in an era when the old urban economy was collapsing, and when self-help and agricultural productivity was the only alternative to helpless starvation or abject submission to slavery and serfdom, dictated Benedict's original insistence upon the obligation to perform manual labor. But whatever the immediate reason, the ultimate effect was to supply something that had been missing alike among the favored classes and the depressed workers in earlier urban cultures: a balanced life, a kind of life

* According to the rule of St Benedict only twelve men were needed to set up a monastery. Now a college of 500 is considered 'unviable'. At the time of writing a DES circular urges the abolition of *'small, uneconomical sixth forms'*.

that had been preserved, though at a low intellectual level, only in the basic village culture. The privations and abstentions imposed by monasticism were for the sake of enhancing spiritual devotion, not to put more goods or power at the disposal of the ruling classes.

Physical work no longer occupied the entire day: it alternated with emotional communion through prayer and plainsong. Here the slave's working day, from sunrise to nightfall, gave way to the five-hour day: with a plenitude of leisure, be it noted, that owed nothing *in the first instance* to any labor-saving machinery. And this new scheme of living was aesthetically enhanced through the creation of spacious buildings, well-tended gardens, thrifty fields. This regimen, in turn, was balanced by intellectual effort in reading, writing, discussion, not least in the planning of the varied agricultural and industrial activities of the monastic community. Shared work had the benefit of shared mind.[7]

We see in the monastery an archetypal image of the good place. It is distressing to find in contemporary papers and publications the word 'monastic' employed to insult and denigrate—for the monastic order was one of the great educational achievements of British history. Distressing, we remark, and yet how typical it is of the pollution of meanings which surround us, and which urges us to call out again for new enclaves to keep at bay the corruption of symbolism and to nourish, once more, the whole life of man. At the same time it must be readily acknowledged that the monasteries were organized around a body of belief which, in its original shape, has become dead and which we cannot hope to resurrect. New enclaves may resemble the physical shape of the monastery, may insist on the need to reunite working, learning and living, but the informing values will be different. As Matthew Arnold predicted in the nineteenth century, the development of the inward man will come to depend more on culture than on formal religion. Also, as other writers of the same century (like William Morris) insisted, the forms of social life must become democratic and not autocratic. In the more recent antecedents to the new college, we will find that these two passions, the passion for culture and the passion for democracy, are by far the strongest.

III

Ruskin College

We turn now to consider one image of a self-managing community.

Ruskin College was founded in 1899 to provide a liberal and residential education for working-class men and women.* The twenty men who came to form the first-year students seemed bewildered by the problem of organizing all the domestic arrangements. They had little experience to fall back on, and presumably, no knowledge of how the older monastic orders were organized. The result was complete confusion and, for a few weeks, no significant study was attempted. Practical problems sapped all the energy! Only those rich enough to employ servants could have the privilege of uninterrupted study—or so it must have seemed to those working-class students in the anarchy of those first fraught weeks. But the confusion provided, in fact, the most potent learning situation as Bruce Forrest reveals in *The Story of Ruskin College*. Indeed, his account is of such interest that we make no apologies for quoting it at length:

---

* In this short account we will concentrate on the democratic experience at Ruskin College in the first years of its life. For those interested in the development of the College we add the following notes.

Although the institute was named after John Ruskin it was founded by an American philanthropist, Walter Vroomen, with the support of another American, Charles Beard. These men named the College after Ruskin for they admired his social and political writings, being particularly attracted by his broad conception of wealth. The College, first called Ruskin Hall, began in 1899 in a house in St Giles Street, Oxford. In 1903 it moved to Walton Street, where it has remained ever since.

The *Oxford Chronicle* described the purposes of the College as they were understood in the last decade of the nineteenth century, as follows:

> The idea of the promoters is to establish an institution where working men of every degree will be able to spend at least one year in Oxford; to put within their reach opportunities of sharing in high branches of education; leisure to pursue such studies as interest them, and a sojourn among elevating and beautiful surroundings.

After three weeks of this [anarchy] the students took charge and provided themselves, as was said, with their first working model of a social contract. A meeting was called and a document entitled 'Regulations for the Domestic Organisation of Ruskin Hall' (popularly known as 'The Constitution') was adopted. Ultimate domestic sovereignty rested with the whole body of resident students, which met from time to time in a 'House Meeting' (the name and the institution, without quite the same onerous domestic responsibilities, still survive in the College); but three managing delegates were appointed as an executive, each holding office for three weeks, and one retiring each week. They were to be responsible for the domestic side and for the preservation of good order, and their responsibilities were jointly to the House Meeting and to the faculty. Jobs were assigned in rotation to the different resident students, and the general

---

Then they may use what they have acquired as they will; but it is hoped that many will go back to their trade, and that the general tendency of the movement will be to implant in the working-classes of England a leaven of men who will bring to their daily work wider minds, and artistic perception.

The College also had an associated Correspondence School which, before the educational experiment had even been started, had enrolled over 400 students. As the institution developed, it received donations from trade unions and working-men's clubs.

In 1907 the students at Ruskin were allowed to attend lectures in the University, although there was often considerable friction between the two institutions. In the same year regular individual tuition, essay-writing and internal examinations, were introduced into the College. In 1920 Ruskin was formally recognized by the state and given an annual grant.

Since the second World War the College has expanded and become something of a model. In 1960, Kivukoni College, a college based on Ruskin and working in close relationship with it, was founded in Tanganyika.

In our account we concentrate on the democratic experience of Ruskin in the early days partly because we believe that the ideas behind modern industrial Socialism have not only ossified, hardened into mannerisms, but also because we believe that they could now, ironically, constitute a threat to mankind. Socialism was a reaction against a capitalist form of industrialism but not against industrialism itself. As we indicate throughout this book, industrialism needs to be questioned.

principle was that all possible domestic work was to be dealt with before ten in the morning or after six in the evening, leaving the middle of the day free for study. One very sound instinct of the new House Meeting was to end the founders' original idea of having two classes of students, one of paying students, who did a little domestic work, and the other of non-paying students, who did more. The House Meeting ordained that everyone should do an equal share, whatever he paid towards his costs. For two jobs, the 'Saturday morning scrub' and that of cook, volunteers were called for at first; but in due time these jobs too were taken into rotation, and the pleasing habit was instituted that the cook had to appear in the doorway of the dining room half-way through the meal to receive the comments of his victims.[8]

The account provides us with an excellent sample of political *paideia*, by which we mean that rare experience of individuals coming together and actually creating out of themselves an acceptable social reality. Here there can be no alienation, for each man has powerfully contributed to the society that arches over his head. The chaos in the first weeks at Ruskin was fertile chaos for it gave birth to a new form of college. That the birth of this college resembled, in many ways, an older offspring of the monastery (for even the 'House Meeting' recalls the daily monastic meeting 'Chapter') in no way diminishes its importance and achievement. And in at least one vital respect, it had gone beyond the monastery—it had placed authority not in one man, the father of the family, but in the family itself. It asserted the principle of radical equality. Each member had an equal say and, therefore, an equal dignity. Obedience was thus transferred from an outside authority to the inner conscience of each person. The meetings were more turbulent and more passionate and, in a political sense, more *real* than any held inside the various monastic orders.

Again, Mr Forrest offers us a lively account of this political education:

It was a capital training . . . It was perhaps a ponderous system; but it had to meet curious conditions. Along with this possible defect, there came in compensation an interest and a value that must be estimated very highly. So much so that the writer, for one, will never regret the experience and the knowledge gained in the course of conducting the business of the house. One saw an institution managed by debate through an assembly, following all the rules of parliamentary procedure. Its members started, in ignorance and without precedent, an entirely new experiment. Their minds were full of political and social thoughts, and theories, and aspirations. Any one who reflects upon all this will see what a *valuable laboratory of political phenomena we created for ourselves*. It was a great lesson to watch precedents in their curious fashion winning a power all of their own, and to notice the final consummation of our reign of law, when the weekly distribution of house duties became an almost automatic deduction from a stereotyped plan, accepted with full confidence as an ultimate and irrefutable authority.[9] [Our italics]

Can any doubt remain that a democratic college should provide through its political meetings an education of that imagination which dares to see new forms and structures to house man's being? And dares not only to see them but to fight for them? In this matter—for even our industrial 'democracy' seems a sham, an abstract vote, a numerical count, a distant conclusion—the early years of Ruskin College* have much to teach us.

IV

The Bauhaus

The overall conception of the Bauhaus and what it accomplished stands as an unsurpassed landmark in twentieth-century education. Founded in 1919 by Walter Gropius, an architect, the Bauhaus began its existence at Weimar, subsequently moved in 1925 to Dessau and later, as a result of suppression by the government of the Third Reich, moved in 1933 to Berlin where, due to continuous interference by the National Socialists, it ended its life. Although it began as a reorganization of the existing art and craft schools in Weimar, it developed to include architecture, which was seen to represent 'the inter-relation of all phases of creative effort, all arts,

---

* It is of interest that after a few years the College did decide to introduce some full-time specialists; some cooks, a caterer, a matron and in due course a domestic bursar. But Ruskin College still retains its House Meeting and a considerable number of domestic and social duties are still undertaken by the residential students.

all techniques'. Through employing some of the finest artists and teachers of the day, it revolutionized the teaching of art and design, and evolved a theory and philosophy of teaching which was subsequently to effect changes all over the world. It re-asserted unity in a time when civilization had become heterogeneous, and art little more than a decoration, made superfluous by mass-production.

Art, design, industry, architecture and craft were seen as related aspects of a single concern. Men, endowed with creative gifts, set to work to change the quality of the cultural environment. In 1919, the year in which the Bauhaus began, Walter Gropius declared in a short but powerful manifesto:

> The ultimate aim of all visual arts is the complete building! To embellish buildings was once the noblest function of the fine arts; they were the indispensable components of great architecture. Today the arts exist in isolation, from which they can be rescued only through the conscious, co-operative effort of all craftsmen. Architects, painters, and sculptors must recognise anew and learn to grasp the composite character of a building both as an entity and in its separate parts. Only then will their work be imbued with the architectonic spirit which it has lost as 'salon art'.
>
> The old schools of art were unable to produce this unity; how could they, since art cannot be taught. They must be merged once more with the workshop. The mere drawing and painting world of the pattern designer and the applied artist must become a world that builds again. When young people who take a joy in artistic creation once more begin their life's work by learning a trade, then the unproductive 'artist' will no longer be condemned to deficient artistry, for their skill will now be preserved for the crafts, in which they will be able to achieve excellence.
>
> Architects, sculptors, painters, we all must return to the crafts! For art is not a 'profession'. There is no essential difference between the artist and the craftsman. The artist is an exalted craftsman. In rare moments of inspiration, transcending the consciousness of his will, the grace of heaven may cause his work to blossom into art. But proficiency in a craft is essential to every artist. Therein lies the prime source of creative imagination. Let us then create a new guild of craftsman and artist! Together let us desire, conceive, and create the new structure of the future,

which will embrace architecture and sculpture and painting in one unity and which will one day rise toward heaven from the hands of a million workers like the crystal symbol of a new faith.[10]

The manifesto was a call for unity, for the reunion of arts and crafts through a single intention, the creation of a whole environment. Elsewhere Gropius talked about building 'the Cathedral of the future'. Behind the demand to create a guild which would draw all the arts together there was a desire to reconstitute the medieval craft-guilds. Even the German word *Bauhaus* (meaning House of Building) bears within it the connotation of the guild-system (*Bauhutte*). In some ways Gropius' appreciation of the medieval cultural synthesis resembles William Morris', yet his response to the industrial age couldn't have been more different. Morris sought to learn from Nature, Gropius from the Machine. Morris evolved a lyrical and organic style, Gropius a functional and geometrical one. The cathedral of the future was to be made of concrete slabs, glass, steel tubes, plastic surfaces, standardized shapes set in geometrical relationship to each other. The demand was for rational purity, a mathematical rigour.

By 1920, the Bauhaus had attracted seventy-eight male students, fifty-nine female students and a distinguished staff which included, then, Moholy-Nagy, Paul Klee and Lyonel Feininger and was soon to include Wassily Kandinsky and Josef Albers.

However, the success of the Bauhaus was directly attributable to Walter Gropius who not only had outstanding qualities himself as architect and teacher but was also able to recognize and gather together artists and teachers of distinction. Although these artists were not united in the method by which the agreed aims were to be accomplished, it was through the integrating genius of the Director that the various parts of the courses were held together and took on general significance. Paradoxically the Bauhaus 'tried to associate individuals with their differing ideas on creative work, without undue direction from above'. Gropius had clearly grasped the pedagogic truth held in Blake's stark aphorism. 'Without Contraries there is no Progression.' It is conflict itself which generates the energy that transcends conflict—a truth most educational institutions, throughout time, have been too timid to face. Although it is true both Itten and Meyer—two fine teachers—had to leave due to their dogmatic adherence to ideas destructive of the overall purpose of the Bauhaus, these were the exception rather than the rule. True education almost always involves a crucial element of risk. If the Bauhaus was safe from the beginning, nothing would have been achieved.

Anni Albers, weaver, and wife of Josef Albers, has written about her early days as a student:

> I came to the Bauhaus at its 'period of the saints'. Many around me, a lost and bewildered newcomer, were, oddly enough, in white—not a professional white or the white of summer—here it was the vestal white. But far from being awesome, the baggy white dresses and saggy white suits had rather a familiar home-made touch. Clearly this was a place of groping and fumbling, *of experimenting and taking chances*.
>
> Outside was the world I came from, a tangle of hopelessness, of undirected energy or cross-purposes. Inside, here, at the Bauhaus after some two years of its existence, was confusion, too, I thought, but certainly no hopelessness or aimlessness, rather *exuberance with its own kind of confusion*. But there seemed to be a gathering of *efforts for some dim and distant purpose*, a purpose I could not yet see and which I feared might remain perhaps forever hidden from me.
>
> Then Gropius spoke. It was a welcome to us, the new students. He spoke, I believe, of the ideas that brought the Bauhaus into being and of the work ahead. I do not recall anything of the actual phrasing or even of the thoughts expressed. What is still present to my mind is the experience of a gradual condensation, during that hour he spoke, of our hoping and musing into a focal point, into a meaning, into some distant stable objective. It was an experience *that meant purpose and direction from there on*. [11] [Our italics]

Annie Albers' fascinating account of the Bauhaus indicates that meaning and form have to evolve through an uncertain process, a quest for what is not clear now but may become so later. No creator—and no educator—begins with perfection. He begins with what is imperfect, confused, strange, enigmatic, seemingly inaccessible. He hopes—but only hopes (for there is no final certainty)—that through the confused struggle, of making and discarding, he may attain the order of enduring art. It is a process of 'gradual condensation' and the most remarkable quality of the

Bauhaus as described by Anni Albers is that the whole fluid institution seemed to embody the rhythms and fluctuations and hopes of the creative process itself. A remarkable accomplishment. Yet the college—or workshop as the teachers preferred to call it—was not a retreat from its own time. On the contrary, it endeavoured to express the purest forms that could derive from an age which emphasized function, utility, and mass-produced shape. It was a search for aesthetic purity in industrial society. It intuitively knew what it was struggling to produce.

Professor Blum, a school inspector, was one of the first to recognize that the Bauhaus was a necessary and significant manifestation of a general historical development. He wrote in a newspaper at the time:

> The question of the Dessau Bauhaus has entered its decisive stage . . . Concerning the matter itself, we must recognise that in this case we are dealing with new ideas which must of course struggle against all the difficulties that are encountered when one introduces something new and particularly something of fundamental importance. We need to ask whether these new ideas are the arbitrary inventions of an individual or a group, are the whim of a more or less ingenious man, or whether as is usual with new epoch-making works of art, they manifest the creative consciousness of the common needs of the time . . . In any case, it seems to me that the essence of the work of the Bauhaus is the pedagogical interpretation of the new ethical problems and educational achievement.
>
> . . . For Gropius and his group it is characteristic that they . . . do not give way to their feelings but instead try to discover the principles of a new style, so to speak scientifically, based on historical and psychological analysis. Except for the obvious differences in temperament, Gropius' attitude to the facts of modern culture may be compared with those of Rousseau. Rousseau recognised the unnatural and degenerate aspects of the playful culture of his environment. In rejecting this culture entirely, he sought for a completely new point of departure for the shaping of life's forms. Hence his call 'Back to Nature!'. Gropius is searching for a new point of departure from the original elements of form, from which an artistic and practical form will result . . . Thus he finds the basic elements for his applied design (*Wegestaltung*). These forms themselves result from the economic and technological situation of the

present day, which presses for standardisation, mechanisation and mass production. This is the reason for his attempt to relate education directly to the crafts and to industry.

Gropius pursued his basic idea with the utmost resolution and almost ascetic rigour. But in this fact lies, in my estimation, the educational significance of his endeavours. He requires absolutely objective work and complete understanding on the part of the craftsmen for the special tasks, and thereby he demands a strong-willed, characteristic way of thinking in respect to the work. His Bauhaus is a laboratory. Hence the concentration on the production of single articles . . . One does not find in the Bauhaus a great quantity of produced goods but what one does find is totally and systematically thought out. The forms which have been found as a result of the present design concept at the Bauhaus are not of essential importance. Some people will not be happy with the plainness and the highly stressed simplicity of the products . . . The Bauhaus reform finds itself . . . in its development phase, at its rationalistic stage. This development will later have its romantic and its classical periods . . .[12]

This commentary written at the time of the experiment in education is extraordinarily perceptive. It not only seizes and formulates the philosophy behind the Bauhaus, it also sees the possible development and evolution of that philosophy. This, the report maintains, was only its first rational stage. It could not remain there forever. Walter Gropius himself had claimed 'only work which is the product of inner compulsion can have spiritual meaning'. The simple original forms made in the Bauhaus would become, in time, mass-produced conventions. What *was* experimental would *become* orthodox. The revolution of yesterday so easily becomes tomorrow's cliché. The recent obsessions for op art, pop art, kinetic art, derive from the Bauhaus. The insistence on function and technique has become empty, trivial and modish, while outside, beneath the tower block flats, under the functional bridges of the motorways and the high and monstrous office blocks, people shift about uneasily, half-paralysed in their planned environments. The young scrawl slogans across the abstract squares and rectangles. An artistic dream has darkened into a social nightmare that few are ready or willing to interpret. What comes after 'rationalization' and 'standardization'? What emerges at the very end of the industrial process?

John Andrew Rice had been during the early thirties Professor of Classics at Rollins College in Florida but, owing to his deep antagonism to the academic reorganization that the college was then insisting on, he was dismissed. His response was to found Black Mountain College. The College had for its premises a fully furnished summer conference centre which, situated among tree-clad mountains, was empty for most of the year. The first term began with nineteen students, mostly from Rollins College, and six faculty members, four of whom had also taught at Rollins and two of whom had also been dismissed. A radical new college was growing out of the hardening shell of the old.

John Evarts in *Black Mountain College* asks 'How did it all start?' and answers:

> In rebellion. First. Then in the attempt to realise a many-sided dream—an ideal college educating the whole person, giving the arts their rightful place as formative, sensitising elements, bringing out latent, but untouched talents, emphasising the individual rather than the mass.[14]

The attack on established practice was not, as it has become in our own time, a cant formula, an essentially nihilistic protest at all institutions and all inherited meanings. It was not iconoclastic. Not egocentric. The rebellion was, rather, the only way to assert the existence of values and the need for new structures which would prompt the development of the true community of individuals. The attack on Rollins College, culminating in the modest founding (nineteen students! six teachers!) of Black Mountain College, was the assertion of a deep belief in the power of education. According to Lewis Shelley:

> The Rollins rebels held two fundamental theses from the beginning: first, that the best development of the individual required that he be trained in relation to wider responsibilities than just himself; secondly, that more than intellectual training was necessary—feelings and emotions must be sensitively disciplined. The means of achieving these goals was to emphasise the creative arts and practical responsibility as equal in importance to development of the intellect, in a community setting where students and teachers lived in close contact with each other. Learning and living were to be intimately connected on a broad base . . .[15]

As we have seen in this chapter, in asserting the value of learning and living, of study and practical responsibility, they were defining for the twentieth century the wisdom embodied in the old monastic system. Black Mountain College, in this sense, was more radical than revolutionary. At the same time it was seeking to reconstitute that communal order in an age without a common faith, without a received morality, without articulate belief in the transcendental. For these reasons, the experiment had to be more difficult, more searching, more fluid, more precarious.

From the outset the College was largely self-sufficient and self-managing. Except for two cooks and, in the winter, a furnaceman, the College had no employees. All the work was divided among volunteers taken without distinction, from both students and staff. In this way, working often side by side, floors were swept, firewood cut, coal shovelled, meals served, clothes laundered, and so forth. In the second year of the College some students decided to start a farm. Under the guidance of one of the tutors a small farm was begun, a farm which was said to supply the members of the community with large amounts of exercise and modest amounts of food. In much the same way as in Ruskin College, the students were being given a social and political education. They were creating their own society and being responsible to it. It is possible to idealize such a community,* but what would seem certain is that the ugly divisions that destroy contemporary society, the schizoid wars between *us* and *them,* blacks and white, staff and students, capitalist and communist, 'hippie' and 'fuzz', parents and children, could not take deep root there so easily—just as they do not grow to any marked extent in traditional village life or in those cultured primitive communities described in the next chapter.

---

* And, no doubt, in reacting against the darkness of our own age, we are guilty of it. We must point out here that there *were* many stormy and bitter faculty meetings at Black Mountain. Over many issues, such as the one as to whether the College should allow black students, there were powerful splits and factions. In a letter describing one of the faculty meetings, a tutor wrote, 'For a while the atmosphere was so dense that breathing was painful.' The tutors and students were often openly divided, but this, however difficult, is, we contend, healthier and infinitely better than the *suppression of intellectual conflict* which characterizes colleges today.

Indeed, in such societies, the community is experienced as an aspect of the self. One simply belongs. Close and daily contact with the other limits the power of paranoid phantasies.

We can see the way in which Black Mountain College in those early years experienced itself as a community by the manner of its response to a challenge that emerged in 1940. In that year it was understood that the College could no longer use the original conference centre. With the aid of funds the College bought a strip of land on the other side of the valley. But there was still no teaching centre, no precious enclave. A large new building had to be erected, with diminishing funds and within the deadline of one year. An ordinary institution would have collapsed under such external pressure. The community at Black Mountain decided to build the large modern building in the afternoons, between the academic studies in the morning and the academic studies in the evening.

John Evarts describes this formidable decision and its educational and practical ramifications at some length:

The decision to do this was made, I think, at a General Meeting of the College, in the early spring of 1940. By autumn, things had begun to be organised when the term began in mid-September. Mr Lawrence Kocher, a distinguished modern architect, and Mr Richard Gothe, a German refugee who had had considerable experience in running work camps in his own country, had been persuaded to join the staff. A professional builder and his assistant were employed to direct the work, and our regular handyman-genius 'Bas' Allen, would be sometimes available. The faculty members and students would be the 'common labourers'. Ted Dreier, the treasurer of the College, had obtained some funds to begin the construction and to adapt the existing summer cottages for year-round use. But not enough to complete the operation, and at first things went extremely slowly . . . It was planned to build a small but beautifully modern and perfect cottage for Dr and Mrs Jalowetz (music). The first steps in preparing for the main studies building, which was to include some sixty studies for students, living quarters for two or three faculty members, class rooms, studios for painters and art classes, were to survey and examine the land. The location chosen was at the end of the lake opposite the dining hall. It was found to be swampy in places and none too solid. Our first jobs were to clear away the bushes and trees, dig drainage ditches, foundation ditches, etc. It was a long, muddy, discouraging, back-breaking job. But we 'common labourers' could at least wield shovels pretty well.

Dick Gothe established teams for the various volunteer workers, and schedules were published daily on the College bulletin board in Lee Hall. Ted Dreier would captain a team of rock-haulers on Tuesday, Thursday and Friday afternoons from 1.30 to 5.30. Jack French (Professor of Psychology) would captain a team to install insulation in the two main lodges, etc. 'Sign here'.

The team I most enjoyed working on was the cement-mixers. I think we may even have had rival cement-mixing teams. With plenty of hands to help, we worked out various would-be efficient systems, taking turns at carrying the heavy wheel-barrows of finished cement to the 'mason's team', taking turns at shovelling the sand into the mixer or hauling the pails of water. As soon as the ground floor began to be formed, the work became more exciting, and little by little we saw the pylons rising, on which the long, boat-like building would rest (pylons that resembled a little the Le Corbusier type). This was the work which amateurs—men and women—could easily do, and I remember the philosophy teacher and psychologist Dr Strauss and the Jalowetzes—their grey hair flying in the breeze—joining my team on some occasions (in Europe, no Dr Professor, I reflected, would be likely to come even near a cement-mixer, let alone carry pails of water!) . . .

The pace of life at Black Mountain College quickened immeasurably that year. The pulses and mind quickened as well. In most cases, the academic work did not suffer, and in many, it may have been livelier and more intense. The more expert workers among the students often spent five afternoons of the week at the jobs, but usually they also fulfilled the demands of their regular studies very well. And the excitement of the operation was infectious.[16]

As Evarts goes on to point out, that the actual work was a necessity to save the college brought an urgency to the task. It was not a 'simulation exercise' invented by a team of professors in order 'to motivate' the students. They were not 'acting out'—the students and staff were confronting a real problem and learning how to work together in order to overcome it. And as life is not divisible, refusing to be broken into hermetically sealed areas, the sense of solidarity developed in the long afternoons of labour and construction, continued to live on in the academic studies and in the general life of the College.

Many of the most vital artistic achievements of modern America originated from Black Mountain College or were, in some way, connected with it: the 'school' of Black Mountain poetry under Olson was directly associated with it and Merce Cunningham's important and highly influential dance company began there. The following is an incomplete list of well-known artists, dancers and writers who taught or studied at Black Mountain or at its Summer Schools: Merce Cunningham, John Cage, Paul Radin, David Tudor, Carolyn Brown, Viola Farber, Robert Rauschenberg, Jasper Johns, Anni Albers, Xanti Schawinsky, Charles Olson, Paul Goodman, Eric Bentley, Erwin Straus, Lyonel Feininger, Ossip Zadkine, Robert Motherwell, Robert Duncan, Kenneth Noland, Gary Snyder, Robert Creeley, Edward Dorn. It was not untypical of Black Mountain College to have together in one performance—for example, Satie's 'The Ruse of Medusa'—such diverse talents as John Cage, Buckminster Fuller, Isaac Rosenfeld, Elaine and Willem de Kooning, and Merce Cunningham. Much as Rievaulx in the twelfth century had drawn into its walls men from all over Europe, so did Black Mountain College act as a cultural centre, drawing to itself some of the most creative and visionary minds of the time.

Lest the reader thinks that with such an extraordinary collection of teachers—and with so many other interests in building and farming—there could have been no sustained and coherent syllabus, we quote the founder's comments on examinations and assessment:

When the student, on consultation with his tutor, thinks that he is ready to graduate, he will submit to the faculty a statement of what he has accomplished and what he knows; if, in the opinion of the faculty, this statement is satisfactory, the candidate for graduation will be required to take comprehensive examinations, oral and written, covering the work he has done in the Senior Division. These examinations will be set by professors from other colleges and universities, and their opinion of his work will be the principal criterion of his fitness to graduate. The use of outside examiners tends to change the relationship of teacher and student, to put their work on a more agreeable footing and increases the student's willingness to work hard.

The purpose of these examinations, to enter the Senior Division and to graduate, is to find out whether the student knows what he professes to know, and how he can use this knowledge. This is one reason why the oral part is considered important, in that it tests the capacity to follow thought in motion. Another is that it is prepared for by intelligent conversation.[17]

There was no question of the students, in today's appalling jargon, merely 'doing their own thing'. The student had to master his own field and be able to demonstrate that mastery to *outside assessors*. There was to be nothing incestuous about the business of evaluation. And yet, for Rice, it was not good enough to rely on the dubious methods of written examination alone. That could encourage all manner of subterfuge and trickery. Only sensitive and testing conversation could reveal whether the student could follow 'thought in motion'. With what contempt Rice would regard the growing practice of computer-marking in our schools, and the ubiquitous tendency to place mechanics before process. Yet with what alarm would he view the vague rhetoric of those who would put in its place an amorphous anarchy, a mindless tolerance of everything. Standards matter. But as Black Mountain College so eloquently demonstrates, those standards, to be meaningful, must relate to a whole education, a process in which hand, heart and mind have come together, been disciplined and, in being disciplined, found a truer harmony.

Once again, we find that the achievement of Black Mountain College, confirms our belief in what is small, what is rooted, what is made (rather than passively received), what is supported by its own energies, and what is taken forward on the momentum of high ideals and a bright vision of cultural possibilities. With the examples of such illustrious antecedents as we have boldly sketched in this chapter at the back of our minds, giving us as it were, moral sustenance, we must move even further back, to consider what we can learn from those primitive cultures which may possess the key to our own future, and then forward to describe more fully the nature of our own college.

III

The Cultural Community

What exists concretely are persons acting in community to create, sustain and enrich a common symbolic world. Call this symbolic world the high culture if you wish, but the activities concerned form a large part of what it means to be human. The central job of education is therefore the care of persons, and a major part of this care is their nourishment through the common symbolic world.

Ben Morris

I

In order to find the philosophical ground for our new college we must dig even deeper. At times in attempting to catch its essential nature we have described it as a cultural and ceremonial centre. We have suggested that its energies would be largely devoted to the creation of forms and the understanding of forms which express concepts of space, time and personal relationship radically different from those of our own age. But even at this point, there is likely to be misunderstanding as to our meaning. Some of our readers will assume from this that we desire to create, perhaps with Arts Council assistance, another place where contemporary poets and artists can seek refuge, a place where, in current jargon, they can go 'mad' and insult, by the creation of anti-art, the society which has rejected them. Nothing could be further from our aim. Such a college does not deserve to exist—and could not last. No community can be built on hate or find itself through the cultivation of mockery, irony and those many techniques which exist only to record utter emptiness and the bleak denial of any route out. Art at the present moment seldom reveals itself as a passionate search for wholeness of being and fullness of life. We live in a state of exile. So far have we travelled from the primary sources of creativity, we have all but forgotten their existence.

As Robert Heilbroner has suggested, the clue to the future may lie buried in the past, in the primitive communities which possessed and nurtured not the anxious skills of material advance but the timeless arts of being-in-the-world. In one sense, we need to go back and not forward: to remember and rediscover rather than 'progress'. In understanding our college—its insistence on democracy, on self-reliance and, above all, its dedication to culture—we too find ourselves returning for inspiration to these communities. T.S. Eliot understood this movement from the civilized to the primitive modes of being in the following way:

> For a long enough time we have believed in nothing but the values arising in a mechanised, commercialised, urbanised way of life: it would be as well for us to face the permanent conditions upon which God allows us to live upon this planet. And without sentimentalising the life of the savage, we might practice the humility to observe, in some of the societies upon which we look down upon as primitive or backward, *the operation of a social-religious-artistic complex which we should emulate upon a higher plane.*[1]

It is this 'social-religious-artistic complex' that we must come to understand for it embodies that unity of existence we have long lost and which, in modest form, and for our own century (because there is no painless shedding of history), the new college would work to resuscitate, albeit as Eliot rightly insists on a higher level.*

---

* It is worth pointing out here that the most significant art of our century has attempted to draw on primitive sources of feeling and identification. At the same time, the artistic achievements—the achievements, for example, of D.H. Lawrence, of Bartok and Henry Moore—remain products of our own age. Henry Moore's sculpture, to take one instance, while expressing primitive energies yet has a refinement of form which is modern. The statue of *Chac Mool,* the Mexican Rain Spirit, which has been the prototype for many of Moore's reclining figures, has a stiff remoteness which disappears in Moore's

To leave the problem here, however, would be evasive. We need to know *what* it is we must emulate upon a higher plane. To say that primitive communities provide a key for the future is consoling but hardly sufficient—for we need to know the shape of that key so that we can recognize and employ it. As we will now try to show, we suspect that the primitive community has much to tell us about the abiding significance of what we call 'the arts' in society. The health of the primitive community may lie in its powers to symbolize and ritualize experience, powers that we have all but lost in our own civilization and which may largely account for its numerous pathologies.

---

transformations. The imagination at work is, in other words, simultaneously modern and primitive. We find this same creative synthesis in the best of D.H. Lawrence's work, in Bartok (who derived so much from folk-culture, still essentially primitive in feeling) and in Stravinsky. Here again we find T.S. Eliot's observations pertinent. In 1923, Eliot wrote about the need to manipulate 'a continuous parallel between contemporaneity and antiquity' in order to give 'a shape and a significance to the immense panorama of futility and anarchy which is contemporary history.' We go back in order to move forward. There can be no question of a simple return to primitive modalities, no question of obliterating the great cultural achievements of Western civilization. The task is one of transformation not regression. The danger is, of course, that it will take the form of regression. The present obsession with 'release', sensation, experience *unmediated by symbolism*, while *seeking* the primitive, yet represents a perversion. Again we can do no better than to quote T.S. Eliot who in the essay *Conformity to Nature* (a title worth noticing) claimed, 'the purpose of re-ascending to origins is that we should be able to return, with greater spiritual knowledge, to our own situation.' Robert Heilbroner is also aware of the difficulty which now confronts industrial man. Will he possess the wisdom to draw only the clear waters from the ancient wells? He writes in *The Human Prospect*, 'What we do not know, but can only hope, is that future man can rediscover the self-renewing vitality of primitive culture without reverting to its levels of ignorance and cruel anxiety.' It will be particularly the task of the arts to show us the way backwards and forwards. In the best of Henry Moore's work we *do* find primitive inspiration and spiritual understanding reconciled. But there remains much to be done, much to be pioneered.

II

In *The Primitive and the Civilized* the anthropologist Stanley Diamond, discussing the place of symbolism in primitive communities, claimed:

> In primitive society, the ritual drama *is* a culturally comprehensive vehicle for group and individual expression at critical junctures in the social round or personal life style . . .
>
> In such ceremonies, art, religion and daily life fuse, and cultural meanings are renewed and recreated on a stage as wide as life itself . . .
>
> These rituals are also creative in the dramatic revelation of symbols and the anticipation and elaboration of new roles for individuals; they make meanings explicit and renew the vitality of the group.[2]

An awareness of the stages of life, an understanding of a constant pattern of birth-growth-death-rebirth, and the need for art and ritual to symbolize the endless process of discarding, adopting and developing would seem to be an essential characteristic of primitive culture. Stanley Diamond has pointed out that Ibo-speaking peoples of Nigeria do not regard a baby as human, *as a member of society,* until it has been given a name at an elaborate ceremony some months after its birth. This ritualistic conferring of a name marks a second birth, recording not the biological birth of the child but the cultural birth of the child into the community. But that is only the first initiation. As the wheel of life revolves, other names are introduced to demarcate and celebrate further powers and responsibilities. Peggy Harper has described the function of dance in Nigerian villages as follows:

> African village dance is what European dance might once have been—an expression of every important stage and event in the life of the individual and the entire society. There are dances for childhood and for old age, for every festival, for every deity, for every major task. The overall style of dancing unifies and identifies the society because every tribe has its own style of dance.[3]

Culture in primitive societies has a direct and intimate relationship to the universal process of psychic maturation. Primitive culture makes visible and therefore accessible the inmost pains, anticipations and hopes of individual life which of itself is most fragile and in the most precarious of states. Huizinga in *Homo Ludens* has expressed the function of primitive ritual as follows:

> Primitive ritual is thus sacred play, indispensable for the well-being of the community, fecund of cosmic insight and social development.[4]

When we compare this concept of sacred play, indispensable for the development of the individual within his community, with the concept of 'leisure time', of colour supplements, television, pop, the general inert consumption of counterfeit objects, we have some measure of contemporary society's exile from the creative centres. And yet, historically, the primitive's dedication to *poiesis* has been the perennial preoccupation of human kind against which our present addiction to technical development and material expansion begins to take on the shape of an immense aberration, a cul-de-sac leading off from the broad track of history.

It was the practice of the first anthropologists living in the first phase of the industrial revolution, to describe man as essentially a toolmaker. On this criterion primitive man was seen to be inferior to civilized man who had advanced so far in the way of tools and techniques. However, the gross inadequacy of this definition of man as technical manipulator has become in recent times all too obvious. Indeed the anthropologists' definition reflected more accurately the assumptions of an industrial culture than it revealed the essential qualities of *man as man*. We know that Neanderthal man not only used simple tools but also that he buried his dead with ceremonial care and in obedience to a powerful archetypal image. Archaeologists have discovered that the dead person was placed by the living in a crouching position and then bound up in the shape of an embryo or an egg, a symbol of resurrection, of rebirth (which still survives in a rather ossified form with our custom of giving Easter eggs). If the use of a flint tool marked man off from the zoological order so did, *and more dramatically,* the custom of ceremonial burial, the shaping of life according to an impelling image, an image which incarnated, furthermore, a belief in rebirth and renewal. The building of forms to mourn, hold and honour the dead—barrow, mound and cairn—are, indeed, the most formidable signs, deposits, rich with meaning, at the gates of history. In brief, there was never only a utilitarian concern for life, there were also visionary and aesthetic concerns, and indeed these concerns were so intertwined they were inseparable.

The cave paintings at Lascaux were drawn and ritualistically stabbed as a preparation for the hunt, a way, perhaps, of luring the bison-spirits near to the cave entrance. Through a trance-like ritual the bodies of the hunters would become taut with concentration and the mind charged with focused energy. Art was thus a preparation for action—for the utile task of securing food. But it would seem unimaginative to conclude that the hunter's culture was only related to killing bison, important as that was. Dr Lommel, responding to some of the later cave paintings, dating from about 12,000 B.C., has concluded:

> If early primitive man was capable of producing such sophisticated works of art with his crude tools of stone and bone, he cannot by any means have been 'primitive' in an intellectual and artistic sense and must, on the contrary, have reached a peak of development that has not since been surpassed.[5]

He draws the disturbing, then liberating, conclusion that *'artistic and mental development does not have to proceed parallel with advances in material civilisation.'* Indeed, we believe that culture and civilization are perhaps finally to be understood as antithetical terms: culture centering on symbol and expression; civilization centering on the signal, the single closed system of unambiguous meanings, and as we argued at greater length in the first chapter, the manipulation of external matter.

Dr Lommel's conclusion is further confirmed by the recent suggestion that Paleolithic man probably hunted, 'worked' as it were, for some fifteen hours a week. What, we ask, did they do for the rest of the time? It would seem reasonable to suppose that they enriched their lives by seeking pattern and poise through the creation of symbolism. They danced, they chanted, they made music. They painted, they carved. They told stories. They invented cosmologies, myths, fables. Indeed they laid the symbolic foundations for all that was to follow: religion, art, science, philosophy. Even the cave which was given by nature *pre-figured* the immense artefacts of the temple and the cathedral where, once again, strange and powerful images were to be painted on dimly lit walls. Lewis Mumford in his classic study *The City in History* describes these first materially impoverished settlements as follows:

> Here in the ceremonial centre was an association dedicated to a life more abundant; not merely an increase of food, but an increase of social enjoyment through the fuller use of symbolised fantasy and art, with a shared vision of a better life, more meaningful as well as aesthetically enchanting, such a good life in embryo as Aristotle would one day describe in the *Politics.* [6]

The image of this the earliest enclave devoted to the good life—the life of cultural transformation—reminds us forcibly of our own proposal for a college and the enduring needs it would seek to satisfy.

The achievement, then, that characterizes man in the pre-historic periods and still characterizes him in all those communities which continued outside of the powerful thrust of conscious civilization points to a nature which is aesthetic and cultural. The desire to create beauty, the passion to find *and* to celebrate an encompassing pattern, a symmetry in which the individual is bound into the wider purposes of the universe, would seem fundamental to man. Nor can there be little doubt that the pursuit of science developed out of the primordial manifold of cultural experience. But in as much as, under the momentum of its own evolution, it has denied the other strands of that manifold: the strand of emotion, the strand of imagery, the strand of relationship in which 'I' and 'it' are found together, in as much as it has denied these strands, it has diminished man and has severed him from the sources of creative energy and spiritual exaltation.

Our cursory examination of the primitive community has unearthed the philosophical key we sought: man is primarily a culture-maker—that is what distinguishes him. He is, as Cassirer worded it, the *homo symbolicum*. It is, we believe, the fundamental denial of this premise and the assertion of other views which see man in the image of the ape or the machine, which has brought so much confusion into our society.

III

Through the creation of the symbol man was able to reel the outside world into his own mind. Through the symbolic process man developed *the power to internalize external objects and to give them further meanings*. Thus, the enormous variety of things in the outside world came to form essential furniture in the house of consciousness. Because man had fashioned images and sounds for the things he had seen, touched, sensed, felt, he could continue *to reflect upon them* and *to possess them* when they were no longer there. He could recall to consciousness what would otherwise have been irretrievably lost.

Furthermore the various internalized objects could relate one to another. Relationships between things could be forged. It is pertinent to note here that the word symbol derives from the Greek word *sumballein* meaning *to throw together,* to join the diverse objects into an imaginative synthesis. The primitives' love of riddles testifies to this delight in the uniquely human capacity to perceive a similarity between objects dispersed in time and context. Poetic language is essentially *metaphoric language* and metaphoric language throws together and fuses the many unexpected relationships between dissimilar objects. It was this energy naturally expressing itself through vivid metaphor which Wordsworth saw as the most obvious gift of the real poet, perceiving 'affinities in objects where no brotherhood exists to passive minds.' It is the power that Picasso affirmed when he inverted a bicycle saddle and left it standing as a bull's head. It is not an important work of art so much as a pictorial maxim celebrating man's genius for recognizing and creating analogies, puns, that talent for *double vision* which divides the human from the animal world.

The second facet of cultural experience which we want to emphasize here concerns a comparable process of transformation but moving in the converse direction, namely *from within outwards*. Through the symbolic process man was able to express—and not only express but give shape to and recognize—the invisible swarm of emotions, images, instincts, apprehensions, which buzzed through the dazed hive of his mind. Through the extraordinary phenomena of speech condensing both meaning and feeling a torrent of unconscious forces could be transformed into quiet pools of reflection in which man could discern his face. Shelley in his *Defence of Poetry* put the matter most succinctly: 'Neither the eye nor the mind can see itself unless reflected upon that which it resembles.'

There would seem to be no tangible access to the mind except through the giant transforming mirrors of art. We discover the lineaments of our own identities by contemplating the artefacts we have made. The symbol is that door which leads into the self and into the self of the other. It is this communication which the philospher Karl Jaspers was referring to when he wrote, 'Alas, we talk so much when what really matters can be stated so simply, not in a universal proposition to be sure, but in a concrete symbol.'[7]

Yet, of course, the division we have upheld between inner and outer is schematic. Its value is analytic not revelatory. What we find, in actual experience and in actual works of art, is the fusion of inward and outward but, and this is important, on the terms of the artist and (in organic cultures) the society he represents. The work of art, in fact, integrates experience so that such divisions as personal-public, inner-outer, subjective-objective, no longer exist. We will have cause to consider the bearing of such unity on the pedagogy of our new college for our general observations on culture carry a rich cargo of suggestions about true modes of teaching. Here we wish to reiterate our central conclusion.

Man, we have argued, is essentially a maker of symbols. Through the creation of words and images, rhythms and gestures, sounds and rituals, he was able to locate a space beyond the narrow realm of the instincts in which another *order of life* could be elaborated, developed and transmitted to others. It was not a question of instinct being denied, so much as it being placed in an infinitely wider structure, the structure of being. The symbol is, thus, the foundation of the human community. We have seen how in the primitive community art knits society together, at birth, at play, at work, at marriage, at death. When the unifying symbol breaks, so imperceptibly does the dignity which should attend our experiencing of the world. Yet we cannot hope quickly or easily to restore such organic beauty as is possessed by whole cultures—even less so in a college, however radical. Such beauty is an immense achievement, it is the labour of ages, of generations living in one place, experiencing one form of life and making it their own through the slow and continuous elaboration of ceremony and rite. What we *can* hope to do, is to prepare the ground, to create space in which cultural (as opposed to material) growth becomes possible, in which society may, however fleetingly, discover itself as a working whole. In the next chapter we will consider the domestic and political aspects of this unity. Here we must continue to reflect on the achievement of culture and the sort of teaching that will be needed if it is to develop inside the new college.

IV

In our college, as in the primitive community, we will attend not to the isolated part but to the meaning and use of the whole. What is used in the college will, where possible, be made by the college. What is made in art will hang from the walls, both in the assembly room where the democratic meetings will be held and in the private recesses where individuals may withdraw for stillness and peace of mind. If chairs and tables are designed, they will be constructed to furnish the lecture theatre, the seminar rooms, and the refectory. If new materials are woven, they will be turned into whatever is needed: curtains, towels, clothes, bedspreads. The best poetry that is written will be heard by the community or skilfully printed. The same with drama, with dance, with music and sculpture. The finer artefacts will become the spiritual objects of the college. It is for the want of a sustained audience, listening and ready to respond wholeheartedly as well as ready to offer discerning criticism, that the arts have turned into sensational bombardments (or ironical withdrawals). The college itself will not only form an initial enclave for the arts, but also, and more positively, provide a community responsive to the creation of new forms. In all traditional societies the artist has been a significant and valued member of his own community. Down to the fifth century B.C. the poet was the educator of the Greek city. In Celtic communities the poet was accorded a very high status. In primitive societies, the shaman, the visionary figure, generally a singer, dancer or artist, the man capable of a journey into the beyond, is still regarded as one who confers psychic health and, as such, is indispensable to the well-being of the community. The college, in the articulation of its general life, will attempt to restore, for our own age and at another level, these ancient traditions.

In the teaching process itself, the emphasis likewise will fall on wholeness of experience and wholeness of response. We will promote an education in which fact, feeling and value are not dissociated; it is vital for man to know what he feels and to feel what he knows. We agree with Coleridge's remark 'deep thinking is attainable only by a man of deep feeling'. Our case for an aesthetic education rests on a further assumption that art, in its proper form, is not a distraction but a concentration of life, a revelation of unified being.* We have shown how this is true in the primitive community. As we shall now see, it is also the way in which the best modern artists have understood their quest.

'*When I create*,' declared the poet Theodore Roethke, '*I am true* and I would like to find the strength to base my life entirely on this truth, on this infinite simplicity and joy.'[8] The process of aesthetic creation discloses an intense and selfless mode of being which the artist would seek to transfer to his own life. Bernard Leach in describing the creation of a pot makes a similar testimony. The clay, as it becomes translated into form and texture, mirrors the whole man—so much so that Leach declares 'the pot is the man, there is no disguise'. Leach has also described this aesthetic experience in terms of Zen Buddhism; it is, he says:

> a state of being attached neither to positive or negative . . . it is a quality we most admire in pots, and it is that rare condition of which we catch glimpses in men and women when the spirit of life blows as through an open window. Then action follows easily, naturally, and without overstress. It's not the outcome of

---

* As we shall show, this does not mean that we shall be concerned only with the arts in our college. An aesthetic education is not to be confined to expressive disciplines; all education, whether it be in the natural sciences or in the humanities, should be aesthetically conceived. *The Philosophy of Science* course (see page 65) will be considered of vital importance in the new college, showing the aesthetic nature of science once it has discarded those mechanical trappings described in Chapter I. As for the humanities, they too will be well represented in our college as can be seen by referring to the syllabus sketched on page 65.

individualism or intellect. It is the possession of the humble craftsman and the haven of the greatest artist.[9]

Here again we find support for our concept of 'whole experience' so absent in today's schools and colleges and so missing from our educational theories.

The marriage of thought and feeling through creative action is not confined to the art forms we have taken our examples from. Dance, properly conceived, is an attempt to articulate through the body moving in space the order of feeling, the structure of unfolding impulse. It is a discipline of creative being. Even the skills of the sportsman at their highest level, are the joyous expressions of the concentrated self. Here, for example, is the way a champion surf-rider describes his sport:

> I've been in the water every day since I was twelve, practising and developing my style. You've got to regulate, moderate, keep refining all the time . . . I'm after perfection—perfect timing, perfect balance, perfect co-ordination—and the perfect wave to try them on. I want to know the waves inside out and be able to control them. After it's over I always feel relaxed. It's a great feeling . . .[10]

With a few superficial changes, it could be a dancer or painter or poet speaking about the process of creation, 'developing style', 'refining all the time', an extraordinary focusing of energy on one event. At the same time, no one would wish to suggest that surf-riding exists on the same level of importance as the fine arts.

In scientific study itself there are strong aesthetic and subjective elements invariably at work, though often submerged and, as we have seen, often denied. Our emphasis on 'whole experience' does not preclude scientific analysis, although many spokesmen for science would be alarmed at our insistence on the union of subjective and objective, affective and cognitive, in their domain. In this realm, above all, we need to assert the need for a comprehensive concept, to insist that even the use of the word 'object' implies a subject and that there can be no science without inward consciousness. Even facts are made by the constructive mind. It is interesting in the light of our earlier remarks on the masculine bias of scientific research, that it is a poetess who makes vivid to us *the beauty* revealed by scientific study. In her autobiography, Kathleen Raine describes how she found more spiritual sustenance in the laboratories than in the poetry circuits of Cambridge University:

> Truth to say there was more of what I meant by poetry in my work in the botany and zoology buildings in Downing Street. There, among flasks and retorts, plant tissues and microscopes and the bones of vertebrates I could still slip off my brave new persona and bathe in nature's healing stream. The marvels of the universe were there open to me and I contemplated in awe and delight the Book of nature . . . As an anonymous student of natural sciences I was more a poet than ever among the Cambridge poets. There my experience was at once aesthetic and magical; those life-cycles and transformations, embryology and morphology, that condensation of force into form which produces 'sensible' nature constituted a harmonious world of significant form indeed.[11]

Here we are left with some inkling of what science, transformed by the concept of wholeness in which subject and object are drawn together by an encompassing energy, would be like.

In the discipline of mathematics Poincaré and Max Planck, the father of quantum theory, remind us of the crucial place of beauty and imagination in mathematical understanding and formulation. Poincaré writes:

> It may be surprising to see emotional sensibility invoked à propos of mathematical demonstrations which, it would seem, can interest only the intellect. This would be to forget the feeling of mathematical beauty, of the harmony of numbers and forms, of geometric elegance. *This is a true aesthetic feeling that all real mathematicians know. The useful combinations are precisely the most beautiful, I mean those best able to charm this special sensibility.*[12]

Max Planck declares that a pioneering scientist must possess 'a vivid intuitive imagination for new ideas not generated by deduction, but by artistically creative imagination'.[13]

These reflections bring us to another crucial observation. We contend that most disciplines properly conceived are themselves significant integrations of knowledge and experience. It is frequently argued today that a broad multi-discipline education is desirable. What often results is merely a superficial education, a 'knowing about' everything and a deep understanding of nothing. The argument for a general education tends to ignore that diverse knowledge and experience are unified and given meaning in many of the traditional disciplines. The discipline of poetry, for example, requires a subtle and extensive knowledge of life. Again we find ourselves quoting Kathleen Raine who, referring to the needs of the contemporary poet, declared:

> You must have built up a great body of knowledge which may include many elements. It may include—I think it should include—*scholarship*; it should include experience of life and death, *science, nature, religion*—whatever goes to make human life. You should be building up. You see, Man has certain maximal possibilities and none of us reach that maximum, but poets, musicians, are, in a way, athletes of the spirit, who are attempting to go a little further, *to advance our humanity somewhat in the direction of what we might become.*[14] [Our italics]

From such diverse knowledge, such multifarious experiencing of the world's many facets, grows a pattern: it takes shape in the poet's mind, a form in which what is known, what is felt, what is imagined, what is sensed, cannot be separated. The poem has an inherent order which is wholly satisfying to contemplate. It is an aesthetic object. At the same time the artefact points in the direction of life from which it has sprung disclosing a unique integration of experience which, through a process of sensitive reading and assimilation, can become the possession of all men. To study poetry is to study the sublime complexities of relationship and understanding as they have been embodied in aesthetic form by the most sensitive and thoughtful minds. It is a distinct and coherent way to study humanity. And the same is true for all the major art forms and for each humanistic discipline.

Such an understanding of the disciplines has important repercussions on the practice of education and the art of teaching. Consider the method of teaching developed by the artist Paul Klee in the Bauhaus, as described by one of his students:

> Actually Klee's teaching was never of the simplest kind, one where the 'teacher' lectures and the 'student' learns. The whole depth of this sphere of ideas and experiences was opened only to those who felt and experienced with him a sphere which is a

systemized reproduction of life in its fullest significance.

In the beginning it was not always easy to follow with complete understanding. But slowly we began to comprehend that someone—Klee—was telling us about life. We were able to experience, together with him, the development of human existence in its entire imaginative range. Together with him, we sped through thousands of years. Klee made us perceptive again to those original experiences that until then had only touched us mechanically. Was this a 'celebration in anticipation of creation' (as an enchanting drawing of Klee's done in 1914, is entitled) which he prepared for us? There was nothing he wouldn't mention. Klee taught us to see the composition and structure of vegetable and animal life. Not only did he teach us to perceive it visually but in his theory of forms he gave us the principles of creativity. He showed us the all-encompassing synthesis which embraces all organic and inorganic life. The very phenomena we were used to seeing in biology and sociology, suddenly became relevant once more in formal design. Everything: zoology, biology, chemistry, physics, astronomy, literature, and typography helped to make us understand (literally) how we, with every bit of our existence and all of our activities, are part of humanity and the cosmic rhythm and how we are engrained in it. Klee taught us the important laws of harmony. Once he said, 'the very last remains a secret, the great silence'. Klee spoke pacing back and forth, or he drew his figures on the blackboard. Then, off and on, he was silent, leaving us time to take everything in.[15]

What was Klee teaching? Which specialist dare say 'art' unless by that term he refers to that comprehensive art of responding to 'the all-encompassing synthesis' of which individual consciousness is an ineradicable part. To study for three years under such an artist would be not only to acquire a rigorous training in technique but (and related to it) a full education in its own right. Nothing could be broader, nothing more integrated than such a course in one discipline.

Let us consider two further examples. At Black Mountain College, Joel Oppenheimer attended the course given by the poet Charles Olson. He described one characteristic session as follows:

The workshops at Black Mountain started at 7.30 and they ended at 9, maybe, or more likely at 12 or 2 or 3. One day the blackboard held four lines, and Charles just kept saying what are they? and I still count it a proud moment, and a good one, when

I said at 9.30: it's a map! And he smiled and said, okay, what map? And a half-hour later we had it nailed down to the Nile, the Tigris-Euphrates, the Danube and the Volga, and we spent the night talking about trade routes and cultural interchanges between the northmen and the south, about the way cultures developed and moved on.[16]

What was the experimental poet discoursing on? The poetry of geography, economics and history.

Even if we move away from the arts and look at the teaching, let us say, of semantics, we find ourselves (providing we discover the inspired teacher) arriving at the same conclusion. In the following passage, John Evarts describes the teaching methods of the founder of Black Mountain College, John Rice:

He would start off with a word or a concept which most people thought they understood perfectly—a word like 'sentimental' or 'democratic' or 'aristocratic' or 'love' or 'honour'. And the discussions on a single concept might continue for two weeks or more—the digressions were enormous; he would confuse the class, showing some of them all too clearly that they didn't say what they meant and didn't mean what they said. He was more than adroit in getting people to speak and in engendering scepticism and caution—he stretched people's minds and made them think. He made them doubt and question the meaning of ideas and concepts which they had blindly accepted. When a word or idea had been scrutinised, dismembered, tossed around for days, interlarded with anecdotes and reminiscences, he would, finally, pull all the loose ends together and by that time his listeners were at least a little wiser and less ready to throw words around which they only vaguely understood.[17]

'Discussions on a single concept might continue for two weeks or more.' How narrow! How academic!—complains the age of 'audio-visual aids' and endless technological stimuli. But as the passage demonstrates, under a great teacher, such a confined examination of a word can engender an educational process as broad as any pursued by Socrates. Indeed Rice's methods, (his habits of questioning, of creating uncertainty, by breaking the fixed patterns of assumed knowledge) as well as his purpose (to arrive at a truth existentially tested) remind one powerfully of the gadfly Socrates. Later in the passage from which we have just quoted, John Evarts admits that sometimes Rice, having broken down a person's certainty, was not always able to build it up again. This again reminds us of Socrates and of those hurt personalities who, feeling publicly humiliated, later engineered his death. It points us also to the extreme risks that attend teaching dedicated to the development of the whole person. What seems certain is that such powerful teaching requires a context, an encompassing framework which provides support and asserts, at all points, the primacy of human values.

We do, however, glimpse in the account of Rice as teacher a sense of how absorbing, demanding, severe and relentless fine teaching is. A good teacher transforms the life of his student. Jonathan Williams described what it was like to be a student of Charles Olson: 'And the conversations were endless . . . Night after night, day after day. He changed my whole poetic vision—and my whole vision of life too'. Endless examples could be quoted. Among the most eloquent testimonies must be that of Eric Gill's, describing the impact of his teacher, Edward Johnston:

> . . . I went regularly to learn writing and to learn about the Roman Alphabet. And I fell in love with Edward Johnston and physically trembled at the thought of seeing him. But he kept me severely in my place and I trembled under his rebukes. I fell in love with him—but don't make any mistake as to my meaning. I fell in love with him as I might, and indeed did, with Socrates. It was a joyful passage. Life was full of physical excitement and the excitement was as of the intelligence discovering the good. It is very well to know the logical truth, but fancy knowing the truth and finding it desirable. More and more desirable and more and more the truth.
>
> I won't say that I owe everything I know about lettering to him . . . but I owe everything to the foundation which he laid . . . He profoundly altered the whole course of my life and all my ways of thinking.[18]

We leave Gill's celebration of the transforming power of great teaching to speak for itself as well as to represent many other accounts of a similar momentous experience of *paideia*, of life itself, under the shaping influence of the teacher, being given form and significance. Once again, we do well to observe that the subject matter is confined (in this case, the art of lettering) but the issues released boundless.

V

We will here summarize our main conclusions concerning the cultural and educational life of the new college. We have argued that:

1. Most disciplines are in themselves significant integrations of knowledge and experience.

2. We therefore suggest that inter-disciplinary studies can best develop meaningfully where the disciplines have been first fully developed in their own right.

3. We have also urged that the approach to learning and creation should be aesthetic. By this we mean that each discipline should seek to elicit a wholeness of response, in which the traditional oppositions between subject and object, feeling and cognition, values and knowledge, are overcome and reconciled in a higher synthesis.

4. We have insisted that the organization of the college (which we will describe in the next chapter) should further support and amplify this quest for wholeness of being.

5. One important way in which this can be achieved is by the members of the college, both students and staff, forming an active community for the expressive arts. The health of all the arts depends upon such a community and, contrariwise, the health of the community depends on the arts. We have seen how a primitive community provides us with a potent image of society living through and being regulated by its own creative symbolism.

6. The importance of each of the foregoing assertions rests on the philosophical foundation that man is not fully comprehended by the partial concepts of 'tool-maker', 'naked ape' or 'reflexive thinking machine' but, rather, by the more comprehensive concept of *animal symbolicum*. As a maker of symbols man transforms his 'natural' world and his experience becomes simultaneously open, unique and irreducibly creative. The power to make culture—and in this we would include not only the arts and crafts but all the disciples of study, including the social and natural sciences, and the many languages on which they depend—constitutes, in the words of David Jones, 'the distinguishing dignity of man' Our college, ultimately, stands on this premise and exists to explore its innumerable implications.

At the same time, the quality of the college will depend on the individual teachers it can draw into its walls. It is of the utmost importance that the best mentors and outstanding artists, poets, musicians, craftsmen, dancers, sociologists, anthropologists, psychologists, cultural historians, philosophers, are attracted to the college, willing to be bound into its communal round. It would be the aim of the college to establish within its first two years, a core of about twenty residential staff, who taken together would represent all the main disciplines in the arts and humanities. It would be axiomatic in such a community that all members of staff would receive the same salary. If the college was validated (as we hope it would be) and the state refused to pay except through the order of hierarchy, then a bogus hierarchy would be set up and the unequal cheques cashed and the money distributed equally (with perhaps some, given the common agreement, feeding the college funds). In a college community demanding a total response from each person, any other system would be intolerable because morally repugnant.

We would hope also to establish other schemes to attract distinguished creators, thinkers and scholars to the college. A system of secondment could be developed whereby professional men and women could be released for short periods, depending on circumstances, for one week, one month, one term, or one year, to give courses at the college. In this way the best and most developed thinking in the outside world would be brought into the college and, in turn, the college would be taken out through the visiting lecturers into the world. Again, it might be possible to establish fellowships which allowed creative individuals in any one of the major fields to reside at the college without any formal teaching commitments. Such schemes would ensure the intellectual vitality of the college and check that inherent tendency of all small communities to become locked within themselves, complacent and self-engrossed.

We hesitate to present an organized curriculum. The college as a whole will form the curriculum, for learning, as we have repeated, will not be confined to the lecture hall or the seminar room. Learning will be taking place on the farm, in the organization of daily life, and, not least, in the weekly democratic assemblies. With regard to the 'academic' curriculum, we would want this to shape itself in relationship to the needs and aspirations of the actual teachers. Socrates had no timetable when he wandered through the small streets of Athens. His teaching followed in the wake of the living and the unrepeatable moment. Individual teachers must make and re-make their own syllabuses according to the needs of specific students and the possibilities opened by specific contexts and specific situations. We must endeavour to elaborate a timetable structure that is flexible, a structure which in every way complements rather than frustrates the essential process of teaching Good teaching requires time, spans of undisturbed time devoted to concentrated study and reflection. We will, therefore, timetable subjects in terms not of hours but of mornings, afternoons and (where requested) days, and, in some cases, of weeks. Education is too important to be hurried, too indivisible to be broken up into sixty-minute pieces, too deep to be constantly interrupted by bells and breaks. Our aim is to penetrate time not to serve it.

The syllabus, in brief, must not be handed down, it must be created through collaborative discussion by all those who are going to teach it. We would hope however to establish within the first few years most of the following disciplines.

Arts	*Humanities*
Arts and Crafts to include:	Philosophy of Science
Painting	Philosophy
Sculpture	Anthropology
Pottery	Psychology
Weaving	Sociology
Metalwork/Woodwork	Cultural History
Printing	Theology
Drama	Ecology and
Dance	Domestic Arts
Music	(in relationship to Farm)
Writing	Literature
Film	The Study of Art

In the first year, subject to agreement by academic staff, the student would be encouraged to submit himself to many of the disciplines listed above in order that he might sense the range of activity available, their various purposes, skills and methodologies. When he later specializes, he will then be able to choose wisely. He will also be able to see his specialism in relationship to the whole pattern.*

In the second year most students would be expected to concentrate their attention on, perhaps, two disciplines. For obvious reasons the details regulating this choice of subjects cannot be given at this stage. Nevertheless it would seem reasonable to suppose that in many cases, the student would be advised to select one area from each column. In this way, he would study for the next two or three years a creative discipline and an academic discipline (both, as we have insisted throughout this chapter, conceived and taught aesthetically).

In the fourth year, those students wishing to teach, having mastered two disciplines, would embark on a one-year 'education course'. We will not describe at length here the nature of this course. Suffice it to say we find ourselves largely in agreement with John Rice who claimed:

---

* It would seem premature to comment at length on this provisional list. However it must be clear to the reader that the list bristles with opportunities for collaborative work. We feel that this should develop from within rather than be imposed from without. Tutors, living within the community, would soon become aware of their affinities and forge the connections they desired between disciplines.

A few further points of clarification are perhaps necessary. By *Cultural History* we have in mind that broad study of culture that is represented, for example, by such works as Lewis Mumford's *The Myth of the Machine*, Ernst Cassirer's *An Essay on Man* and Susanne Langer's *Philosophy in a New Key*. Such a course could be developed in close relationship to the *Philosophy of Science* course which, again, would be broad in scope and sympathetic to that creative concept of science developed, for example, by Marjorie Grene and the symbolic philosophers. The psychology studied would tend to concentrate on psycho-analysis and on existential psychotherapy. The sociology would likewise have a humanistic perspective and perhaps concentrate on the possibilities of phenomenological research. Again, these disciplines of enquiry might well choose to collaborate on pieces of research or even develop a common syllabus. Finally we must point out that the *Ecology* and *Domestic Craft* courses, working in close relationship with the college farm, would be indispensable to the community's goal of self-sufficiency and self-management. This will be discussed more fully in the last chapter.

Teaching is a secondary art. A man is a good teacher if he is a better something else; for teaching is communication and his better something else is the storehouse of things he will communicate. I have never known a master in any field who was not also a master teacher.[19]

Having mastered both a creative and an academic discipline, our student is already more than half-prepared to teach. In the last year of his course he must experience plenty of teaching-practice (in the schools and also in the college, taking first-year seminars); he must become aaware of current educational thought; he must, also, develop a coherent pedagogy relating to his own discipline(s). The latter suggestion requires, perhaps, a little further elaboration.

Today it is common practice to discard rigorous methods of teaching and to promote, in their place, a happy and naively tolerant approach to all things. There are courses in abundance which, while demanding no standards, blithely promise to make a poet, potter or composer out of any one and every one in a matter of weeks, days, or even hours. These infinitely tolerant methods (further disseminated by publishers, with such titles as 'Pottery is Easy', 'Fun with Maths', 'Creative Sequin Stitching') make no discrimination between noise and music, between mere expression and concentrated form, between collective cliché and personal revelation. There is no such thing as instant art or if there is, it is not worth having. Art is a discipline of the whole being, it depends for its vitality and spontaneity on the mastery of techniques and a sensitive and ever deepening awareness of tradition. The teaching of the arts in this country is, for the most part, without fitting pedagogies. We lack a native and systematic grammar for each art form. We also lack the knowledge of how and when to present that grammar in the schools. Kodaly's system of music training,* offering a comprehensive and ordered programme from childhood onwards, provides one example of the sort of organized pedagogy we have in mind, Martha Graham's approach to modern dance**

---

* This system of music training, developed by the composer Zoltan Kodaly, is used in the schools in Hungary. It begins as soon as possible with singing games. 'Singing,' wrote Kodaly, 'is the instinctive language of the child, and the younger he is the more he requires movement to go with it. The organic connection between music and physical movement is expressed in singing games. These, particularly in

the open air, have been one of the principal joys of childhood from time immemorial.' (quoted in *Education for Teaching* Summer 1971). The aim of these early games, often employing folk songs, is to develop a strong and natural feeling for rhythm and harmony. In this manner the inward ear is developed and a sensitive musical literacy developed. Instrumental playing does not begin before the age of seven and profits from the early preparatory work. At all points, emphasis is laid on the best, traditional and modern, and spurious forms of music such as that expressed by 'the top twenty' carefully excluded. It is pertinent to our theme that Kodaly himself saw music as at once an aesthetic and a moral discipline. His comment 'Thinking in parts is thinking of others, this is what harmony means' has, simultaneously, a musical and a human meaning. For a succint description of the Kodaly method see Cecilia Vajda's article *The Kodaly Way of Music Education* (*Education for Teaching*, Summer 1971).

** The new discipline of dance promoted by Martha Graham in America developed exercises and movements which first explored the dancer's relationship to the ground and then progressed towards the liberated mastery of all space. This pure form of dance dispensed with the special apparatus of classical dance with its pointe work, its elaborate costumes and sets and returned to bare or nearly bare feet with which the dancer maintained a closer and truer contact with the ground. To say the new dance—the modern American dance—is pure, is not to say it is abstract, for it retained a link with ethnic and Greek dance and sought to express human mood. But the dancer had the courage to forego reliance on traditional dance form, on costume, on props, theme and, sometimes, even music, so that the body had no distraction from its primary aesthetic purpose. His 'being in the world' became a display celebrating and enacting the liberation of man.

The new dance created by Martha Graham and Merce Cunningham is one of the most extraordinary cultural achievements of recent decades. To watch Cunningham or members of his company is to see dancers performing marvellously at the boundary of human possibility and control, placing themselves at high aesthetic risk, at a critical level of personal honesty. Cunningham worked with Martha Graham, and his own classes incorporate what is known as Graham technique but at the same time add another dimension—the spontaneity and self-discipline of the dancers themselves.

Our new college must have such dance at the centre of its life. In Britain we have a small number of people who share this mature and dynamic concept of dance. The new college could provide a permanent and sustaining base from which a group of dancers could work and teach.

another. The lack of coherent teaching-methods in the arts suggests an important task for our own college. In that fourth year, working in intimate liaison with the surrounding schools, tutors and staff could begin to develop a body of materials and methods to foster an ordered training in the arts.

The college's strong commitment to the training of teachers would urge the community to look outwards as well as inwards. The schools would come into the college; the college would go out into the schools. In this gentle manner, through numerous exchanges, the idea of the college would be dispersed. It would pass from the college into the schools, from the schools into the society. And if the seeds of the idea are good, being the reproductive agents of a strong plant, they will find soil and grow. In the last analysis, the curriculum of the college which we have here outlined exists (as a strong seed exists also) to secure the future.

In the final chapter, we will describe how the college will become partly self-sufficient and largely self-managing. During the last decade, it has become transparently clear that only a society which conserves and cherishes nature's produce can survive. This has important implications for educational theory which have still to be properly defined. We will try now to show what some of these implications are, and how they will affect the practical day-to-day running of our college.

IV
The Self-Managing Community

In short, the sharing of work experiences, the sharing of citizen responsibilities, and the sharing of the full cycle of family life, in homes and communities that are themselves re-dedicated to these values—this is part of the constant discipline of daily life for those who seek to transform our civilization. Without this balance in our daily activities, we shall not bring to our larger task the emotional energy and the undistorted love—not crippled by covert hatred and compensatory fanaticism—that it demands.

Lewis Mumford

I

Examining the three major external threats to human life, the threat of nuclear war, of increasing population and of environmental pollution, Robert Heilbroner in *An Inquiry Into the Human Prospect* concluded:

Unlike the threats posed by population growth or war, there is an ultimate certitude about the problem of environmental deterioration that places it in a different category from the dangers we have previously examined. Nuclear attacks may be indefinitely avoided; population growth may be stabilized; *but ultimately there is an absolute limit to the ability of the earth to support or tolerate the process of industrial activity, and there is reason to believe that we are now moving toward that limit very rapidly.*[1] [Our italics]

According to this analysis, and it is one that many ecologists confirm, the central challenge is to curb industrial production, and, therefore, the habits of consumption, on which urban life depends for its thin sense of identity. In the 'underdeveloped' world cities are doubling in size every ten years. People are deserting the countryside, drawn by a counterfeit image of material affluence—of cars, cosmetics, deep-freezes, television sets, alcohol, and gadget upon gadget—an affluence which has become impossible because unsupportable. The multitudes cannot, even if it were desirable, live out the advertisements. As we have remarked before, the physical world is closing in on us. The ever-increasing demand for more, has merely uncovered nature's finitude, those limits within which we exist.

The crisis before us demands qualities and values antithetical to those prevalent today. Habits of waste must be converted into habits of thrift; habits of mindless excavation into habits of mindful preservation; a life of neurotic consumption into a life of joyous frugality. Many have argued that such a conversion will not take place willingly, but through the cruel power of necessity, through war, devastation, plague and through the repressive regimes of military dictatorship. It would be foolish to be optimistic. Yet it would be inhuman not to fight for the decent path, not to hope that the conversion could happen peacefully, through the feelings of mutuality, through the medium of the imagination.

We have considered elsewhere in this book the psychological and cultural nature of the necessary transformation of man. We must now consider one further aspect, namely that of work and economics. The needs here would seem to be fourfold:

1. To restrict production to genuine needs.
2. To develop methods of production which do not require the massive use of non-renewable resources.
3. To develop forms of production which provide enjoyable occupation for the makers.
4. To keep the units of production relatively small in scale and democratic in structure and close to the surrounding community.

In this chapter we wish to explore first the general educational implications of our position and, finally, its implications for the practical running of the new college.

II

Work, and by this we mean all those tasks essential to the creating of an abundant life, should be an integral concern of colleges and schools. Our concern can no longer be to fit individuals into the existing order, the technological meritocracy of mass-society has released into its own bloodstream the poisons that will destroy it. For the majority of people, work has become little more than a passport to a colour television and a deep-freeze. In our society, work has become that long period in which living is postponed, in which one waits for five o'clock, for Friday afternoon, for the summer holiday, for retirement, for an abstract wage-packet. Adolescents leave our schools largely unprepared for the experience of futility that awaits them and even less prepared for the humiliations that may confront them as soon as they become employed, or, as likely, unemployed. Since birth, they will have been fed with the ceaseless propaganda of the advertising trade and, during the last few years at school, been coaxed by careers advice of dubious merit. But most of the young will never have been given a chance to sense how work in itself can be wholly absorbing, infinitely satisfying and essential to the good life. Perhaps, then, it should become our aim as teachers to hold out to those otherwise destined for the typing pools, the production lines and the dole queues, a dignified alternative. Perhaps we should transmit to the young, skills they can master, as well as a simple knowledge of how to make such basic products as bread, cheese, furniture, utensils, clothes. This cannot be dismissed as 'romantic' for it provides a wholly *practical training*. Nor does such training exist in a complete vacuum. There is, even now, in the making a series of serious experiments across Britain, exploring the possibilities of intermediate technology, of mixed organic farming, of small-scale industries based on local materials and needs. These fragile experiments prefigure the ecological society that will, sooner or later, with an uncertain movement, emerge out of the cracked shell of industrialism.

Because schools have failed to respond critically to the consumer society, much of education is dedicated to tackling pseudo-problems, superficial problems invented by 'educationists' to keep children occupied. Schools are, quite simply, not aware of economics; they have become too detached from fundamental life-sustaining activities. Life in school is not lived, it is, in the appropriate American jargon, 'simulated'. No wonder children gaze out of the glass windows dreamily waiting for the bell or, more defiantly, cut their names into the desks provided by the Welfare State.

By suggesting that schools are uneconomic, we do not mean to imply that schools must be regulated according to the dictates of a crude cost/benefit analysis. Far from it! By 'economic', we refer to that energy in man which creates what it genuinely needs and which sees that the common wealth (as once defined by Ruskin) is fairly and lovingly distributed. Nor in advocating work as an integral part of the curriculum do we mean the production of ashtrays, scones, book-ends and pipe-racks. In schools today many girls do learn to cook meals and boys often make coffee-tables, but these products and artefacts do not generally arise out of the actual daily needs of either the school or the surrounding community. The school meals are not arranged and cooked by the staff and pupils. Nor, to take another example, is the school furniture designed and made and repaired by the woodwork department (as has happened in Cuba).

Yet we have only to observe young children to see how much they desire to imitate the daily tasks of 'adult' life. Here, once again, we have much to learn from Coleridge who claimed that 'children are much less removed from men and women than generally imagined'. In the home, at the age of three or even younger, children want to wash up, use a pan and brush, dust, make cakes, make beds, lay the table, write, post letters, wash clothes, light fires. Outside they want to garden, cut and nail wood, build, pass tools, collect vegetables, feed chickens and collect eggs. Children who are allowed, with due care, to tackle these tasks, thereby develop skills and powers of co-ordination and have no need of so-called 'educational toys'. At the same time work provides a fitting means by which the child can enter into relationships with the adults about him. Through being allowed to work, the child discovers himself as an indispensable member of the human community.

We should dispense with pseudo-problems in education and replace them with real tasks. This is not to deny the creative powers of phantasy and play in a child's life. Nor is it to undermine the intellectual and aesthetic strivings of the human mind. These, as we have maintained throughout this book, are of crucial importance. What we are arguing is that imaginative and intellectual activities should be the essential concerns of a community which can support itself and is, therefore, strong and autonomous. We also want to insist that aesthetic and intellectual energies attend the making of a table or a dress, just as practical energies attend the making of a poem or a piece of sculpture. We are loath to make sharp divisions between 'pure arts' and 'applied arts' or, for that matter, between 'economies' and 'academies'. Our quest is for wholeness.

It is interesting to note here that, for a variety of reasons, both noble and ignoble, work has often been recognized, particularly during the eighteenth and nineteenth centuries, as a valuable part of schooling. By most accounts the introduction of 'work' into the curriculum invariably leads to an improvement in 'academic' performance. In Chapter Two we saw that this was also the case with some of our antecedents. Karl Marx, who was so opposed to the exploitation of labour in the nineteenth century, yet believed that 'if the element of exploitation could be removed from it, then child labour ought to become an essential part of education'. After the Soviet Revolution a small group of teachers in Russia drew up an educational programme which stated: 'The personality shall remain as the highest value in the socialist culture'. It went on to claim that the personality can only develop its natural inclinations in a harmonious society of equals, whose actual solidarity of interests is based on a stable community. The school would thus be transformed into a

> working commune based on self-activity, on productive labour for common use and adapted to local conditions. The School should not be opposed to life, but coincide with it, and should endeavour to create a harmoniously developed human being.[2]

To support such ideals is not to approve of the socialist industrial state. Like Western society, Russia has also effaced local communities, 'liquidated' the peasantry, fostered meritocratic class distinctions, and betrayed, if it ever possessed, the concept of the good place and the good life. Like America and Europe, Russia imperialistically asserts values which are culturally blind, ecologically ignorant and spiritually impotent. State socialism and capitalism are rooted in the same impoverished soil of materialist philosophy: it is not surprising they are so similar and have come to understand and reflect one another. Quite simply they are variations on the one exhausted theme of unlimited industrialism, of endless economic growth.

Gandhi also saw the educational value of labour and opened schools in India and South Africa based on the principle of self-reliance. He saw that it was wrong to run schools as 'charities' in which children learnt to waste or disregard things that others had made. He declared:

> I have made bold, even at the risk of losing all reputation for constructive ability, to suggest that education should be self-supporting. By education I mean an all-round drawing out of the best in child and man—body, mind and spirit. Literacy is not the end of education, not even the beginning, it is only one of the means. I would begin the child's education by teaching it a useful handicraft and enabling it to produce from the moment it begins its training.[3]

There is nothing utilitarian about Gandhi's proposal. It is not made by the materialist who would return us to 'solid objects', 'hard facts', 'market statistics'—it is made by one who sees education as a 'drawing out of the best' and comprehends that as a total process of 'body, mind and spirit'. Gandhi's assertion that literacy is *one* of the means of education and that hand-work and the creation of artefacts is equally important, has been affirmed by many other distinguished thinkers, prophets and artists. On one of those many occasions in which he discussed education, Albert Einstein said 'I should demand the introduction of compulsory practical work. Every pupil must learn some handicraft'.[4] The same had been demanded by D.H. Lawrence, by Herbert Read, and before them, by William Morris, John Ruskin and William Cobbett. A similar philosophy of work has also been propounded in America, in the works of, for example, Lewis Mumford, Paul Goodman, John Rice, John Dewey and Henry Thoreau. The principle has an impressive ancestry. Nor has it remained only a principle. In a number of places it has been converted into reality. The imaginative energy that clusters round a living principle has crystalized into social form.

In Denmark a new college, democratic and self-managing, has been recently established. According to one account:

Students become self-reliant and self-disciplined by working with staff to plan their own work programmes. Decisions are taken jointly, often after long argument and discussion and everyone has to face the consequences of their own ideas or behaviour . . . As well as running the schools, the Tvind group also provide or run facilities which the student groups and others can use. These include a fully equipped bus and motor repair shop, and a printing workshop where the schools' textbooks, songbooks and pamphlets are produced. There are also, of course, all the normal things you would expect in a large school—a sports hall, library, music room.

One difference is that the staff and the present students have helped to build the place from scratch. They have worked on the foundations, the drains, the central heating and the wiring of buildings. They have planted trees, laid roads, put on roofs, done carpentry and painted. It gives them a great sense of identity with the school.

. . . At the moment the group are building the biggest windmill in the world to provide hot water and central heating for all their buildings and greenhouses. They are very popular locally and have had no difficulty in convincing the local authority to accept their ambitious plans. It is a scheme which is typical of the group and no more improbable than their plans for transforming teacher training seemed when they first put them forward a few years ago.[5]

In North Vietnam there is emerging an education not unlike the one which Gandhi proposed and not unlike the one being pioneered in Denmark. One school at Hoa Binh, fifty miles west of Hanoi, is now completely self-supporting after twelve years of existence.

In 1962, with the school hardly constructed, teachers and pupils reclaimed 400 hectares of land from the jungle and set up an industrial complex designed to process raw products: cassava, peanuts, mangtang seeds, into flour, vermicelli, sauce, oil and alcohol. This is an excellent laboratory for practical exercises accompanying science lessons . . . it is actually a school organised according to a new formula: study combined with work. Its only goal is to train the young people and cadres *to study well*. The production work, which serves to maintain the school and its staff and students, *makes theoretical studies more lively* and closely connects them to the realities of life.[6]

In our own country Rudolph Steiner schools have long recognized the need for crafts and the direct production of food and other necessities. The Peredur Home School in Sussex, for example, is a supplier (well known in the area) of excellent milk, yoghurt and bread, while at the same time it produces meat, eggs and vegetables for its own table. Good weaving, pottery and wood-turning are also produced and bring in extra income. These opportunities are seized upon by the severely maladjusted children, who are justifiably proud of themselves at being so gainfully employed. It is in the skilled making of objects that children in our schools could once again experience the delight of creation, the pleasure of co-ordinating hand, heart and mind in the production of needed artefacts. One of the reasons why Karl Marx so rightly attacked the division of labour was that it caused the worker to regard the result of his toil as an alien thing, something over which he had no control and which therefore robbed him of the energy he had put into it. It is clear, he wrote,

> that the more the worker spends himself, the more powerful the alien objective world becomes which he creates over against himself, the poorer he himself—his inner world—becomes, the less belongs to him as his own . . . He puts his life into the object, but now his life no longer belongs to him but to the object.[7]

In the primitive society, from which, as we have argued, we have so much to learn, and even in the small village to this day, the artefact is admired for expressing the identity of its maker and often remains a treasured object within the community. Such creation confers dignity to the worker but it demands, at the same time, hours of absorbed labour and an integrated mass of knowledge. George Sturt in *The Wheelwright's Shop* gives a sharp picture of the craftsman's experience:

> We got curiously intimate with the peculiar needs of the neighbourhood. In farm-waggon or dung-cart, barley-roller, plough, water-barrel or what not, the dimensions we chose, the curves we followed . . . were imposed upon us by the nature of the soil on this or that farm, the gradient of this or that hill, the temper of this or that customer or his choice perhaps in horseflesh . . . What we had to do was to live up to the local wisdom of our kind; to follow the customs, and work to the

measurements, which had been tested and corrected before our time, in every village shop across the county . . . The work was more of an art—a very fascinating art—than a science.[8]

It was an art, moreover, that bound the maker into the community whose wants he served. Here, again, we do well to remind ourselves that much work in primitive and in traditional societies is not a solitary affair but a social event, accompanied by song, ritual and conversation. If we are told always of the 'hardness' of life in the old countryside let us not deny it (for why should life be 'easy'?) but let us, simultaneously, point to the sense of festivity which attended it and which we, alas, have long since lost. The Irish playwright, J.M. Synge, gives us one example in his book *The Aran Islands*, which he visited in 1907:

> Like all work that is done in common on the island, the thatching is regarded as a sort of festival. From the moment a roof is taken in hand there is a whirl of laughter and talk till it is ended; and, as the man whose house is being covered is a host instead of an employer, he lays himself out to please the men who work with him.
>
> The day our own house was thatched the large table was taken into the kitchen from my room, and high teas were given every few hours. Most of the people who came along the road turned down into the kitchen for a few minutes, and the talking was incessant.[9]

In such descriptions, and this must stand for many, we discern a society in which the arts of symbolization are unconsciously cultivated; where life attains the order of ritual; where work, so essential to survival, is yet not a matter of 'killing time' but of employing it to enhance the life of all. 'The talking was incessant'—those badly housed and underprivileged peasants possessed a standard of living which our industrialized proletariat have yet to dream of. Paradoxically such descriptions, even as they pull us back in time, yet take us forward. They point to an alternative future. The habit of remembering has become a subversive activity.

III

In our college the students will be asked to pioneer a true form of

PROPOSAL FOR A NEW COLLEGE 79

democracy, a democracy which dispenses with hierarchy and which refuses to depend, like all state institutions of learning, on a hidden proletariat. The college will employ no middle-aged servants to wait on the young at table, no servants to clean boots, make beds, dust rooms, no old women will scrub the stairs and corridors as students pass by holding their books, discussing Marxism. We find the Oxbridge traditions in this respect quite offensive. How can the intelligent young, who still seem to move from Oxford and Cambridge into the BBC, the Civil Service, the Houses of Parliament, know what democracy means when, even before their adolescent pimples have disappeared, they are waited upon like monarchs and popes? When, even as teenagers, they are taught an aristocratic division between leaders and led, between the imperious and the submissive? The practice of employing a proletariat, openly, as at Oxbridge or covertly, as elsewhere, perpetuates an ugly division between man and man, a division which no real democracy could tolerate. For this reason, staff and students in the new college will be expected to organize and regulate, as far as possible, their own domestic affairs. And, as we have already said, there will be no difference of salary between the staff. And no hierarchy artificially imposed.

Let us look a little more closely at the labour employed by the higher institutions of education. An existing college of education for 800 students—about half of whom are resident—employs the following 141 administrative and domestic staff:

1	bursar
1	deputy bursar
5	domestic bursars and assistants
21	secretaries, typists and clerks (including library staff)
1½	telephonists
1	catering officer
1	assistant catering officer
11	cooks
60	domestic assistants (cleaners, waitresses, dishwashers)
1	head gardener
9	gardeners
10	technicians (science, drama, art, maps, audio-visual aids, outdoor activities)

5	handymen or porters
2	drivers
2	painters
2½	nurses
2	security officers
1	engineer
3	assistant engineers
1	lodgings officer

Total 141

Taking into account the number of students who reside out of college it is possible to arrive at a ratio of one non-teaching staff member to every four or five students. This is nearly two for every one member of the academic staff. This is not only costly* but, on the education principles we have developed in this book, absurd. Why shouldn't academic staff and students run their own library? Have the pleasure of tending the communal gardens? Have the responsibility of driving their own vehicles and organizing their own equipment? And, finally, the burden of sweeping their own floors? Of these 141 administrative posts, we might only wish, at the outset, to keep half-a-dozen: we might, for example, need a bursar, a farmer (who would be a teaching member of staff), a cook (who would be closely connected to the Domestic Arts course), an engineer and a secretary. All the rest of the work would be done by members of the college according to rotation and request, fairly established at the weekly democratic assembly.

---

* Some indication of this cost can be gleaned from the following figures for expenditure on education in the year 1972-73:

Teachers	£'000
Primary	453,726
Secondary	491,787
Further Ed.	218,529
Other Staff	428,202

Cleaners, cooks, gardeners, technicians are clearly a major and, for the most part, quite unnecessary expense. (Figures taken from *Times Educational Supplement*, 23.5.75.)

The practical work of the college could be divided under the following headings:

1. *The essential personal services of students and tutors:* meals, cleaning of rooms, washing of clothes, bed-linen, etc.

2. *Work on the production of food:* The college would have its own farm, its own kitchen gardens and its own orchards. Not every student would be required to work on the farm or in the gardens (except perhaps at harvest time). A number of students, probably many of those studying the Ecology and Domestic Arts course, would work at the farm on a regular basis and according to an agreed work-rotation. The college farm, as well as providing the main bulk of the food for the staff and students, would thus be part of a training course in organic farming.

3. *The other work necessary for the running of the college:* maintenance, drains, water, fuel and power supplies, library, bookshop, bar, care of the grounds and gardens, secretariat, guests, nursing, accounting, supervision of all waste products for recycling, crèche, accident prevention, fire precautions and security.

4. *The further work necessary for the college's growth towards self-reliance:* This would entail the transmission to students of a theoretical and practical knowledge of many skills and processes including: breadmaking, the action of yeast, milling of cereals, brewing, distilling, food preservation by drying, salting, smoking, pickling etc, manufacture of dairy products and allied animal husbandry, animals kept as an aid to art and science studies, natural energy sources, elementary building construction, printing of college journals, programmes etc, manufacture of clay utensils, wool carding, spinning, weaving, dyeing etc.

Students and tutors would have to form groups to perform part of the total work load. But in a concentrated physical environment—a natural curiosity would tend to make everyone familiar with the work of everyone else. Tutors would work alongside students in many tasks, probably putting in fewer hours but not exploiting their status to avoid commitment. Task changes might be made at termly, half-termly, or yearly intervals, or not at all. Changes might be made at any time by mutual agreement. In all matters it would be essential to make sure that definite responsibilities had been explicitly allocated. Surprisingly, having to perform a fair amount of physical, domestic work does not detract from, or lower the standards of the academic work—in fact, as we have seen in our study of Black Mountain College, the opposite tends to occur.

It would not, we feel, be too difficult to find a building fitting the practical and residential requirement of our new college. Indeed, many of the small colleges, now being closed or run down, would provide ideal sites. First of all, these traditional colleges of education, built in the nineteenth century, are the right size. They have generally been designed according to the Oxford/Cambridge collegiate pattern which, in scale, resembles our own. Secondly, a good number of these colleges still possess a variety of solid out-buildings, excellent storage space (for the preserving of food and fruit) as well as a laundry and, sometimes, a bakery. Thirdly, some of them still hold a considerable acreage of land, gardens, orchards, woods and fields—which would be essential for farming and gardening. Finally, recent capital investment in these colleges has meant that they provide excellent teaching and lecturing areas, lecture halls, drama studios, art studios, libraries and so forth. These buildings, now becoming empty as a result of administrative vandalism, ask to be used again, to harbour new life, to support the fresh concepts of education now tentatively emerging.

It would be tedious to offer here further lists and possible methods of rotation and organization. In our antecedents, in the monastery, in the early years of Ruskin College, in Black Mountain College, we have pointed to thriving examples of largely self-managing communities. They have worked in the past and there is no reason why they should not work again in the future. After the present phase of industrial civilization has passed away, a social order, resembling in certain economic respects the monastic order, may well reappear. There can be little doubt that, as with science, we need to draw economics back into a wider framework of human reference. Economics cannot be divorced from the concept of communal need and the reality of the individual's conscience. In one sense, our college exists to assert that marriage or, rather, remarriage—for the medieval world had seen and sanctioned the union of morality and economics. However, the terms and possibilities of that union will be, must be, profoundly different from those engendered by the great monasteries. It is within the enclave of the new college that those terms and possibilities, hinted at throughout this book, must be tentatively formulated and not only formulated but celebrated.

In the relentless effort to articulate common purposes and shared values the meeting will be of crucial importance. The meeting is the regular coming together of a whole community with a sense of seriousness and dedication in all that matters to it. The meeting is the place where any issue relating to the practical and communal life of the college can be raised and openly discussed. More fundamentally still, it is the place where the fine art of communication—the art of speaking and of remaining silent, the art of encouraging individuals to overcome their self-doubt and shyness—is developed and refined. Walt Whitman claimed that democracy was a great word but one whose true meaning still slept within our imagination. In the regular college meetings, we would wish to reawaken the true meaning of the word. We define democracy as *the equal participation of all in the affairs of the community*. No one would argue that such a democracy is easy to achieve but it is made infinitely less difficult in the context of the small self-reliant community created out of a sense of purpose and out of a critical response to its own age. In such a community the problems of everyday domestic life would provide the tangible subject-matter for common discussion, and out of the prolonged discussions a common pattern of references and assumptions would emerge, giving the college an intellectual and moral cohesion. We know that at Black Mountain College, in critical periods, the community meetings were as painful as they were long but at other quieter periods the same meetings fostered a rapt closeness and a warm unanimity of purpose. Such a unanimity, not denying conflict and, indeed, often arrived at through conflict, our college through its regular meetings would seek to create. Democracy would thus become an intimate experience of all within the college, not an occsional event and an abstract counting of numbers.

Out of such democracy, out of the experience of shared work, both practical and academic, both domestic and creative, meanings will develop. Out of meanings, ceremonies. In this way we may find again the old balance and the symbolic language of the arts come to express once more a common wisdom and a common discipline. The new theme for man's mind may begin in prose but it should culminate in poetry.

IV

We would like, finally, to draw together the main threads of our argument, adding, as we do so, a few further details.

Ideally, we see the new college set in the countryside or in a small town. The buildings that house our experiment must possess the ordered rhythms and generous proportions of good architecture. They should provide both the convivial spaces for the main communal meals and meetings as well as more solitary areas for reflection and intimacy. The college should be in or near to an expanse of open countryside, perhaps near mountains and forests, or near the sea or a river estuary or rolling farmlands, where the spirit of man can take flight. We find ourselves agreeing with Thoreau who claimed: 'The prospect of a vast horizon must be accessible in our neighbourhood, where men of enlarged views may be educated. An unchangeable kind of wealth, a *real* estate'.[10] At the same time, the college should not be too far from an urban centre offering good museums, libraries and a variety of schools for teaching-practice. Indeed, we believe the college should have in the nearest city a small residential annexe where tutors and students could more readily make use of the urban resources. Here they would also be reminded of the harshness of many people's lives. For it is not our wish that members of the college should be protected from the realities of modern industrial and commercial existence.

Although the new college will, as we have argued, experience itself as deeply opposed to the dominant and frenetic trends of our time, it will yet not be a narrow place cultivating the habits of withdrawal. On the contrary, while much of traditional value would find a home there, the college would be anxious to send out its runners to take root in the cracks and the crevices of industrial society. Its concern with ecology, with aesthetic education, with fresh political and social structures, its commitment to self-reliance, all of these emphases mark it off from most other contemporary educational institutions which seem so impotent before the great crisis which now confronts humanity. The college is not a negative withdrawal from but a creative response to the present state of society. It exists to nurture the new.

The success of the college will depend on the teachers it can attract. It is crucial that they can inspire and develop the talents of the young. They would have to be able to manage a dual task, to teach their own academic or creative discipline and to be able to contribute to the communal and domestic life of the college. They would all receive equal pay, be of equal status and be responsible for electing their own faculty chairman. At the same time we must bear in mind that even the most talented peoples can be 'human, all too human'. Ailred of Rievaulx realized this in the twelfth century and made it a creative part of his own psychology and pedagogy. The new college, like the old monastery, would have to try to learn—and learn painfully—from the many inevitable failings that would accompany its growth.

Aesthetic education, primarily through the arts and humanities, would lie at the heart of the college curriculum. Each discipline would develop its own structure and then explore the possibilities of collaboration. In a small college these connections would grow spontaneously. There would be no need to set up committees. If material circumstances permitted it, the human sciences and perhaps even the natural sciences, would develop in importance. But the human dangers of expansion would have to be assiduously watched and considered. All the courses of the college would need to secure validation. This may prove difficult but we do not think it would be impossible, for the fact that the running costs of the college would be *half* those of any other comparable institution should appeal to a sympathetic local authority, or, failing that, an individual patron.

So, we modestly ask for one experimental college, a college which will raise the banner of meanings and values above the complex of industrial and functional institutions in which the human spirit has been so quietly, so insidiously, and so efficiently extinguished. We believe that all schools and colleges should come to emulate the new college, becoming smaller, more democratic, more cultural, and more self-reliant. In this way, and perhaps only in this way, can the post-industrial society of the future be peacefully inaugurated.

References

Chapter I

1 Advertisement for London Polytechnic in *Dip. H.E. News*, 1974.
2 *The Times Educational Supplement*, 14 March 1975.
3 Open University Prospectus, 1971.
4 L.C. Knights in 'Do our Training Colleges Bear Scrutiny?', *Scrutiny*, December 1932.
5 Nicholas Bagnall in *Fit to Teach*, edited by Bruce Kemble, Hutchinson Educational, 1971.
6 Charles Darwin in *Autobiography*, edited by Nora Barlow, Collins.
7 W.B. Yeats in *A Vision*, Macmillan.
8 W.B. Yeats from *Fragments, The Tower, Collected Poems*, Macmillan.
9 Robert Heilbroner, *An Inquiry into the Human Prospect*, Calder & Boyars.
10 ibid.

Chapter II

1 Lewis Mumford in *The Transformations of Man*, Harper Torchbook.
2 Walter Gropius, *The Listener*, 16 October 1969.
3 Walter Daniel, *Life of Ailred*, edited by F.M. Powicke, Nelson.
4 ibid.
5 ibid.
6 David Knowles, *Saints and Scholars*, Cambridge University Press.
7 Lewis Mumford, *The Myth of the Machine*, Secker and Warburg.
8 Mr Forrest quoted in *The Story of Ruskin College*, Ruskin College, 1949.
9 ibid.
10 Walter Gropius in *Bauhaus Manifesto*, quoted in Dennis Sharp's *The Bauhaus*, Visual Publications.
11 Anni Albers, *On Designing*, Weslyan University Press.
12 Professor Blum in *The Bauhaus*, edited by Wingler, M.I.T. Press.
13 Walter Gropius, *The Listener*, 16 October 1969.
14 John Evarts, 'Black Mountain College: The Total Approach', *Form* no 5, 1967.
15 Lewis Shelley, 'The Founding of the College', *Form* no 4.
16 John Evarts op. cit.
17 John Rice, 'Black Mountain College: A Foreword' *Form* no 5.

Chapter III

1 T.S. Eliot in 'Conformity to Nature', *Selected Prose*, Penguin.
2 Stanley Diamond in *The Primitive and the Civilized, Tract 18*, The Gryphon Press.
3 Peggy Harper in *Radio Times*, 29 November 1975.
4 J. Huizinga, *Homo Ludens*, Palladin.
5 Andreas Lommel, *Prehistoric and Primitive Man*, Paul Hamlyn.
6 Lewis Mumford, *The City in History*, Penguin.
7 Karl Jaspers in *The Challenge of Existentialism: A Symposium, Tract 16/17,* The Gryphon Press.
9 Bernard Leach in the film *A Potter's Life*, BBC TV, directed by John Read.
10 Midget Farrely, quoted by Craig McGregor in the *Observer*, 13 October 1963.
11 Kathleen Raine, *The Land Unknown*, Hamish Hamilton.
12 Quoted in Arthur Koestler, *The Act of Creation*, Picador.
13 ibid.
14 Kathleen Raine in *The Poet's Calling*, op. cit.
15 Hans Wingler in *The Bauhaus*, M.I.T.
16 Joel Oppenheimer, *The Village Voice*, 15 January 1970.
17 John Evarts, *Black Mountain College*, op. cit.
18 Eric Gill in *Autobiography*, Jonathan Cape.
19 John Rice quoted in Paul Goodman's *The Community of Scholars*, Random House.

Chapter IV

1 Robert Heilbroner, op. cit.
2 C. Rosenberg, *Education and Revolution*, *International Socialism*, 49, 1971.
3 Gandhi, *Democracy: Real and Deceptive*, Navajivan Publishing House.
4 Einstein quoted in Moszkowski, *Conversation with Einstein*, Sidgwick & Jackson.
5 Margaret Murray in 'All the Skills in the World', *The Times Educational Supplement*, 22 August 1975.
6 General Education in the D.R.V.N. 1971.
7 Karl Marx quoted in *Readings in Sociology*, edited by Burns, Penguin.
8 George Sturt in *The Wheelwright's Shop*, Cambridge University Press.

9   J.M. Synge, *The Aran Islands*, Dent.
10   H.D. Thoreau in *Thoreau's World*, edited by C.R. Anderson, Prentice-Hall.

Bibliography*

Books relating to Chapter I

1. *On the Failure of Education and Mass-Culture*
Abbs, Peter, *The Black Rainbow*, Heinemann Educational Books.
   Root and Blossom, Heinemann Educational Books.
   The Politics of Education, A Symposium, Tract 10/11, The Gryphon Press.
Arnold, Matthew, *Culture and Anarchy*.
Betsky, Seymour, *Towards a Critique of Industrial Culture, Tract 15*, The Gryphon Press.
Eliot, T.S., *Notes Towards the Definition of Culture*, Faber and Faber.
Holbrook, David, *The Masks of Hate*, Pergamon.
   English in Australia Now, Cambridge University Press.
Henry, Jules, *Culture Against Man*, Penguin.
Inglis, Fred, *The Imagery of Power*, Heinemann Educational Books.
Jones, David, *Epoch and Artist*, Faber and Faber.
Leavis, F.R., *Nor Shall My Sword*, Chatto and Windus.
Robinson, Ian, *The Survival of English*, Cambridge University Press.
Skolimowski, Henryk, *Ecological Humanism*, The Gryphon Press.
Thompson, Denys, *Discrimination and Popular Culture*, Heinemann Educational Books.
Williams, Raymond, *Culture and Society*, Penguin.
   Communications, Penguin.

2. *On the Rise of Science and the Decline of Culture*
William, Barret, *Irrational Man: A Study of Existential Philosophy*, Heinemann Educational Books.
Cassirer, Ernst, *An Essay on Man*, Bantam Books.
Grene, Marjorie, *The Knower and the Known*, Faber and Faber.
Hudson, Liam, *The Cult of the Fact*, Liam Hudson.
Mumford, Lewis, *Art and Technics*, Columbia University Press.
   The Pentagon of Power, Secker and Warburg.
Polanyi, Michael, *Personal Knowledge*, Routledge and Kegan Paul.
Poole, Roger, *Towards Deep Subjectivity*, Allen Lane/Penguin Press.
Read, Herbert, *Ikon and Idea*, Faber and Faber.
Roszak, Theodore, *Where the Wasteland Ends*, Faber and Faber.
Spengler, Oswald, *The Decline of the West*, Alfred Knopf.
Small, Christopher, *Science and Belief, Tract 8*, The Gryphon Press.

Books relating to Chapter II

Duberman, M., *Black Mountain: An Exploration in Community*, Wildwood House.

Evarts, John, 'Black Mountain College: The Total Approach', *Form* no 6, 1967.

Fairfield, Roy P., *Teacher Education: What Design?*, Antioch College Report, 1967.

Gandhi M., *Basic Education*, Navajivan Press.

Gasquet, Abbot, *English Monastic Life*, Methuen.

Gropius, Walter (ed.), *Bauhaus 1919-1928*, Branford.

'In Conversation with George Baird', *The Listener*, 16 October, 1969.

Grote, Ludwig, Contribution to *Bauhaus Exhibition Catalogue*, Royal Academy, 1968.

Hedden, Mark, 'Notes on Theater at Black Mountain College 1948-52', *Form* no 9, 1969.

Harding, Stephen, *Carta Caritatis*.

Jaspers, Karl, *The Idea of the University*, Peter Owen.

Jaegar, Werner, *Paideia, The Ideals of Greek Culture,* Oxford University Press.

Knowles, David, *Saints and Scholars*, Cambridge University Press.

Leavis, F.R., *Education and the University*, Chatto and Windus.

Meiklejohn, *The Experimental College*, Harper, New York.

Merton, T., *The Waters of Silo*, Sheldon Press.

Newman, J.H., *The Idea of a University*.

Rice, John Andrew, 'Black Mountain College: A Foreword', *Form* no 5, 1967.

Riesman, D., *Constraint and Variety in American Education*, University of Nebraska Press.

Ruskin College, *The Story of Ruskin College*, Ruskin College, 1949.

Rykwert, Joseph, 'The Dark Side of the Bauhaus', *The Listener,* 3 September, 1968.

Sanford, Nevitt (ed.), *The American College*, Wiley.

Schawinsky, Zanti, 'Black Mountain College: Spectodrama, Play, Life, Illusion', *Form* no 8, 1968.

Shelley, L., 'The Founding of Black Mountain College', *Form* no 4, 1967.

Thompson, E.P., *William Morris: From Romantic to Revolutionary,* Merlin Press.

Wingler, Hans, *Bauhaus*, M.I.T. Press.

Zabriskie, George, 'Black Mountain College: A Personal Memoir, 1944-5', *Form* no 5, 1967.

Books relating to Chapter III

1. On Primitive Culture

Bowra, C.M., *Primitive Song*, Mentor.

Diamond, Stanley, *The Primitive and The Civilized*, *Tract 18*, The Gryphon Press.

  In Search of the Primitive, Transaction Books, New Jersey.

Elwin, Verrier, *The Tribal World of Verrier Elwin*, Oxford University Press.

Huizinga, J., *Homo Ludens*, Palladin.

Langer, Susanne, *Philosophy in a New Key*, Mentor Books.

Lommel, Andreas, *Prehistoric and Primitive Man*, Paul Hamlyn.

Mumford, Lewis, *The Myth of the Machine*, Secker and Warburg.

  The City in History, Penguin.

2. On the Creative and Academic Work of the College

Abbs, Peter, *Autobiography in Education*, Heinemann Educational Books.

Arnheim, Rudolf, *Towards a Psychology of Art*, Faber and Faber.

Bantock, G.H., *Education, Culture and the Emotions*, Faber and Faber.

Buber, Martin, *Between Man and Man*, Fontana.

Cassirer, Ernst, *An Essay on Man*, Bantam.

Collingwood, R.G., *The Principles of Art*, Oxford.

Ehrenzweig, Anton, *The Hidden Order of Art*, Weidenfeld and Nicolson.

Eisenstein, S., *The Film Sense*, Faber.

Erikson, E., *Childhood and Society*, Penguin.

Gandhi, M.K., *Basic Education*, Navajivan Pub. House.

Gill, Eric, 'Abolish Art and Teach Drawing', *Athene*, Journal of S.E.A., March, 1941.

Goodman, Paul, *The Community of Scholars*, Vintage/Random House.

Holbrook, David, *Human Hope and the Death Instinct*, Pergamon.

  The Exploring Word, Cambridge University Press.

Hourd, Marjorie, *The Education of the Poetic Spirit*, Heinemann Educational Books.

  On Creative Thinking, *Tract 13*, The Gryphon Press.

Leavis, F.R., 'English—Unrest and Continuity', *The Times Literary Supplement*, 29 May 1969.

Mills, C. Wright, *The Sociological Imagination*, Oxford.

Milner, Marion, *On Not Being Able to Paint*, Heinemann Educational Books.

Morris, Ben, *Commentary to Paper by G.H. Bantock*, Butterworths.

Oakeshott, N., 'Education: the Engagement and its Frustration' in *Education and the Development of Reason*, ed. by Dearden, Hirst and Peters, Routledge and Kegan Paul.

Pateman, Trevor, *Counter Course,* Penguin.

Pelz, Werner, *The Scope of Understanding in Sociology*, Routledge and Kegan Paul.

Read, Herbert, *Education through Art*, Faber and Faber.

Schiller, Friedrich, *On the Aesthetic Education of Man*, Oxford University Press.

Sheets, Maxine, *Phenomenology of Dance*, University of Wisconsin Press.

Steiner, Rudolf, *The Essentials of Education*, Rudolf Steiner Press.

Vajda, Cecilia, The Kodaly Way of Music Education, A.T.C.D.E. Education for Teaching, Summer 1971.

Walsh, William, *The Use of Imagination*, Chatto and Windus.

Walsh, William, 'Dialogue and the Idea' from Black Paper on Education, *Critical Quarterly*, 1969.

Wilkinson, E. and Willoughby, L.A., Introduction to Schiller's *On the Aesthetic Education of Man*, Oxford University Press.

Winnicott, D.W., *The Maturational Processes and the Facilitating Environment*, Hogarth.

Playing & Reality, Hogarth.

Books relating to Chapter IV

Benedict, Ruth, *Pattern of Culture*, Routledge and Kegan Paul.

Bonhoeffer, Dietrich, *Life Together*, SCM Press.

Brecht, B., 'On the Everyday Theatre' (poem) in *The Great Art of Living Together,* Granville Press.

Buchanan, Keith, *Reflections on Education in the Third World*, Spokesman Books.

Goodman, Paul, *The Community of Scholars*, Vintage/Random House.

Heilbroner, Robert, *An Inquiry into the Human Prospect*, Calder and Boyars.

Kohr, Leopold, *The City as Convivial Centre, Tract 12*, The Gryphon Press.

Kropotkin, P., *Mutual Aid*, Allen Lane.

Fields, Factories, Workshops, Allen & Unwin.

Maurice, F.D., *Learning and Working*, Oxford University Press.

Morris, William, *Political Writings*, Lawrence and Wishart.

Mumford, Lewis, *The Conduct of Life*, Secker & Warburg.

Ruskin, John, *Unto This Last*.

Schumacher, E.F., *Small is Beautiful,* Abacus.

Sturt, George, *The Wheelwright's Shop*, Cambridge University Press.

---

*   All Gryphon Press pamphlets and monographs can be obtained from The Gryphon Press, 38 Prince Edwards Road, Lewes, Sussex.

Acknowledgements

The authors and publishers wish to thank the following for permission to quote copyright material: The *Times Educational Supplement* for 'All the Skills in the World' by Margaret Murray; Calder & Boyars for the extract from *An Enquiry into the Human Prospect* by Robert Heilbroner; Ruskin College for the extract from *The Story of Ruskin College*, revised third edition 1968, available from Ruskin College, Oxford; The MIT Press for the extracts from *Bauhaus*, ed. Hans Wingler; M.B. Yeats, Miss Anne Yeats and The Macmillan Co. of London and Basingstoke for the extract from 'Fragments' from 'The Tower' from *Collected Poems*; Secker & Warburg Ltd for the extract from *The Myth of the Machine*; Oxford University Press for the extracts from Walter Daniel's *Life of Ailred*, ed. F.M. Powicke; Wesleyan University for the extract from *On Designing*, copyright © 1961 by Anni Albers; Mrs W. Gropius for the extracts from the article by Walter Gropius in *The Listener*, 16.10.69, and for the extract from the *Bauhaus Manifesto* by Walter Gropius.

We are grateful to Kate Carey for advice and support, particularly during the early drafts of this book.